DEMYSTIFYING
THE
PROPHETIC
STUDY MANUAL

Shippensburg, PA

DEMYSTIFYING
THE
PROPHETIC
STUDY MANUAL

UNDERSTANDING THE VOICE OF GOD FOR THE COMING DAYS OF FIRE

JOSEPH Z

Published by Harrison House Publishers

Shippensburg, PA 17257

ISBN 13 TP: 978-1-6675-0604-3

ISBN 13 eBook: 978-1-6675-0605-0

For Worldwide Distribution, Printed in the USA

1 2   3   4   5   6 / 27 26 25 24

CONTENTS

Letter from Joseph 7

Section One   **The Voice of God** 9

One   The Voice of God from the Mountain. 10

Two   Conversations in Heaven. 20

Three   Multidimensional God 25

Four   The Prophetic Spectrum—The Four Types of Prophecy. 31

Five   Prophetic DNA—Witchcraft or Legitimate? 40

Six   Encounters with the Spirit 44

Section Two   **Navigating and Interpreting the Spirit Realm.** 49

Seven   The Map and the Territory 50

Eight   A Better Hermeneutic—
Revelation, Interpretation, Application 57

Nine   Two Prophecies, One King 69

Ten   *Sensus Plenior*—Deeper Fuller Meaning 75

Eleven   The Mystery of Appointed Times and People 84

Section Three   **Dark Powers and Strange Encounters** 92

Twelve   Gatekeepers to the Spirit Realm 93

Thirteen   Mysteries and Strange Happenings 99

Fourteen   Angels of Light and Doctrines of Demons 110

Section Four   **Rightsizing the Prophetic** 123

Fifteen   Harnessing the Experience 124

Sixteen   The Counterfeit Anointing 136

Seventeen   False Prophets. 146

Section Five   **Agents of God** 162

Eighteen   Encountering Prophets 163

Nineteen   Office of the Prophet 168

Twenty   A Prophet's Reward 181

Twenty-One   De-institutionalizing a Revelation 192

                Dear Reader 201

                About Joseph Z 203

LETTER FROM JOSEPH

Prophecy is a tremendous gift manifested by the Holy Spirit and functions today under the New Covenant. In its pure form, prophecy is a gift because of what it contains for the recipient. When properly engaged, the gift is an experience with God's Voice, perfect love, clarity, prediction, and even warning.

> *For prophecy never came by the will of man, but holy men of God spoke as they were moved by the Holy Spirit.*
>
> —2 Peter 1:21

Prophecy does not manifest by the will of man; instead, it operates first through holy men of God who were moved along by the Holy Spirit—holy men are still moved by the Holy Spirit today.

This same Holy Spirit *prophetic unction* was the catalyst of inspiration by which the Holy Spirit brought forth the written Word of God. Therefore, the gift of prophecy and Scripture were not meant to operate independently of one another. The two cannot be separated without a healthy operation of the gift. Prophecy will cause the Word of God to come alive in a revelatory manner and is a tool that brings great value. Through clear training and understanding, with a biblical foundation, the prophetic should always lead to its ultimate purpose: to bring glory to Jesus!

Prophecy testifies of God's great care for you. Prophecy predicts the future and speaks to the heart. It breaks chains and brings encouragement and edification. It is to be desired more than the other spiritual gifts and holds a uniqueness for every believer that is worth exploring. There are countless testimonies from countless people throughout history who are forever impacted by the Voice of God because they had an encounter with the prophetic.

For all the blessings and controversy surrounding the prophetic, it is one of God's greatest gifts to His people. Through it, the magnificence of His Voice and love for His children is shown. The prophetic has made a lifelong impact on me. Since I was nine years old, I have had tremendous encounters through experiencing the various aspects of what I call the prophetic spectrum. At that time, there was no training within my reach to help me walk through my experiences, which ultimately induced a desire to understand these unique occurrences and their purpose. It was a path of discovery through the Word of God that led to this book and manual. It results from many years of study, practice, experience, and rightsizing through God's Word.

This manual is to help you take what you have read in *Demystifying the Prophetic* and go deeper with the Lord. There are focus points and personal reflection moments in each chapter. Please take your time as you work through these. Be honest and allow the Holy Spirit to minister to you while you review each question in this book. I certainly don't know all there is about prophetic—it is, however, my desire to share with you some of the things I have learned along the way. With the Holy Spirit as our Guide—I believe together, we can *Demystify the Prophetic!*

Let's start the journey!

For Jesus,
Joseph Z

SECTION ONE

THE VOICE OF GOD

CHAPTER ONE

THE VOICE OF GOD FROM THE MOUNTAIN

SCRIPTURES

1. **First Samuel 3:4-7**— That the Lord called Samuel. And he answered, "Here I am!" [5] So he ran to Eli and said, "Here I am, for you called me." And he said, "I did not call; lie down again." And he went and lay down. [6] Then the Lord called yet again, "Samuel!" So Samuel arose and went to Eli, and said, "Here I am, for you called me." He answered, "I did not call, my son; lie down again." [7] (Now Samuel did not yet know the Lord, nor was the word of the Lord yet revealed to him.)

2. **Exodus 19:18**— Now Mount Sinai was completely in smoke, because the Lord descended upon it in fire. Its smoke ascended like the smoke of a furnace, and the whole mountain quaked greatly.

3. **Exodus 24:16**— Now the glory of the Lord rested on Mount Sinai, and the cloud covered it six days. And **on the seventh day He called to Moses out of the midst of the cloud.**

4. **Hebrews 12:18-21**— For you have not come to the mountain that may be touched and that burned with fire, and to blackness and darkness and tempest, [19] and the sound of a trumpet and the voice of words, so that those who heard it begged that the word should not be spoken to them anymore. [20] (For they could not endure what was commanded: "And if so much as a beast touches the mountain, it shall be stoned or shot with an arrow." [21] And so terrifying was the sight that Moses said, "I am exceedingly afraid and trembling.")

5. **Psalm 138:2**— I will worship toward Your holy temple, and praise Your name for Your lovingkindness and Your truth; for **You have magnified Your word above all Your name.**

6. **Proverbs 8:12-31 KJV**— **I wisdom** dwell with prudence, and find out knowledge of witty inventions. [13] The fear of the Lord is to hate evil: pride, and arrogancy, and the evil way, and the froward mouth, do I hate. [14] Counsel is mine, and sound wisdom: I am understanding; I have strength. [15] By me kings reign, and princes decree justice. [16] By me princes rule, and nobles, even all the judges of the earth. [17] I love them that love me; and those that seek me early shall find me. [18] Riches and honour are with me; yea, durable riches and righteousness. [19] My fruit is better than gold, yea, than fine gold; and my revenue than choice silver. [20] I lead in the way of righteousness, in the midst of the

paths of judgment: [21] That I may cause those that love me to inherit substance; and I will fill their treasures. [22] **The Lord possessed me in the beginning of his way, before his works of old.** [23] I was set up from everlasting, from **the beginning,** or ever the earth was. [24] When there were no depths, I was brought forth; when there were no fountains abounding with water. [25] Before the mountains were settled, before the hills was I brought forth: [26] While as yet he had not made the earth, nor the fields, nor the highest part of the dust of the world. [27] When he prepared the heavens, I was there: when he set a compass upon the face of the depth: [28] When he established the clouds above: when he strengthened the fountains of the deep: [29] When he gave to the sea his decree, that the waters should not pass his commandment: When he appointed the foundations of the earth: [30] Then I was by him, as one brought up with him: and I was daily his delight, rejoicing always before him; [31] Rejoicing in the habitable part of his earth; and my delights were with the sons of men.

7. **Hebrews 12:29**— For our God **is** a consuming fire.

8. **Exodus 19:19-24 KJV**— And when the voice of the trumpet sounded long, and waxed louder and louder, Moses spake, and **God answered him by a voice.** [20] And the Lord came down upon mount Sinai, on the top of the mount: and the Lord called Moses up to the top of the mount; and Moses went up. [21] And the Lord said unto Moses, go down, **charge the people, lest they break through unto the Lord to gaze, and many of them perish.** [22] And let the priests also, which come near to the Lord, sanctify themselves, lest the Lord break forth upon them. [23] And Moses said unto the Lord, the people cannot come up to mount Sinai: for thou chargedst us, saying, set bounds about the mount, and sanctify it. [24] And the Lord said unto him, Away, get thee down, and thou shalt come up, thou, and Aaron with thee: **but let not the priests and the people break through to come up unto the Lord, lest he break forth upon them.**

9. **Second Samuel 6:6-7**— And when they came to Nachon's threshing floor, **Uzzah put out his hand to the ark of God and took hold of it, for the oxen stumbled.** [7] Then **the anger of the Lord was aroused against Uzzah, and God struck him there for his error; and he died there by the ark of God.**

10. **Luke 2:8-14**— Now there were in the same country shepherds living out in the fields, keeping watch over their flock by night. [9] And behold, an angel of the Lord stood before them, and the glory of the Lord shone around them, and they were greatly afraid. [10] Then the angel said to them, "Do not be afraid, for behold, **I bring you good tidings of great joy which will be to all people.** [11] For there is born to you this day in the city of David a Savior, who is Christ the Lord. [12] And this will be the sign to you: You will find a Babe wrapped in swaddling cloths, lying in a manger." [13] And suddenly there was with the angel a multitude of the heavenly host praising God and saying: [14] "Glory to God in the highest, and **on earth peace, goodwill toward men!**"

11. **John 10:10**— I have come that they may have **life,** and that they may **have it more abundantly.**

12. **John 14:8-9**— Philip said to Him, "Lord, show us the Father, and it is sufficient for us." [9] Jesus said to him, "Have I been with you so long, and yet you have not known Me, Philip? **He who has seen Me has seen the Father**; so how can you say, 'Show us the Father'?"

13. **Hebrews 1:3 KJV**— Who being the brightness of his glory, and **the express image of his person**, and upholding all things by the word of his power, when he had by himself purged our sins, sat down on the right hand of the Majesty on high.

14. **Second Corinthians 4:4 KJV**— In whom the god of this world hath blinded the minds of them which believe not, lest the light of the glorious gospel of **Christ, who is the image of God**, should shine unto them.

15. **Colossians 1:15 KJV— Who is the image of the invisible God**, the firstborn of every creature.

16. **John 10:27 KJV**— My sheep hear my voice, and I know them, and they follow me.

17. **Luke 17:26-30**— And as it was in the days of Noah, so it will be also in the days of the Son of Man: [27] They ate, they drank, they married wives, they were given in marriage, until the day that Noah entered the ark, and the flood came and destroyed them all. [28] Likewise as it was also in the days of Lot: They ate, they drank, they bought, they sold, they planted, they built; [29] but on the day that Lot went out of Sodom it rained fire and brimstone from heaven and destroyed them all. [30] Even so will it be in the day when the Son of Man is revealed.

18. **Revelation 19:10**— Worship God! For the testimony of Jesus is the spirit of prophecy.

As you read each chapter of *Demystifying the Prophetic*, each section will include some questions to think about and space to write down your answers and thoughts.

GOD DESCENDED UPON THE MOUNTAIN

Imagine it, if you would, the God of heaven and earth accessible in the natural realm with signs and wonders! What do you think your reaction would have been on seeing this sight?

_____

_____

_____

_____

_____

_____

THE VOICE OF GOD TORE INTO THE NATURAL

When thinking about being in this setting, I don't think there would be the right words to describe the awestruck crowd and the fear that settled in each heart. It could have been complete silence or maybe a gasp from the mouths of the trembling group.

What do you think your response to hearing the audible Voice of God would have been?

_____

_____

_____

_____

The presence of the Lord was so intense, pure, holy, and powerful, the people begged that the word should not be *spoken to them anymore!* This experience must have been so terrifying to the people that they begged for it to stop.

Have you ever had a moment in your life when you didn't want to hear the Voice of the Lord or His Word?

_____

_____

_____

_____

How could these people get to the point where they were afraid of the One who delivered them from bondage? In your previous answer, what was the situation that made you feel you didn't want to hear the Voice of the Lord or His Word? Be honest, this is a tough question.

_____

_____

_____

_____

HIS WORDS CARRY POWER!

God gave us His words and will, a direct extraction of His supernatural world, and made it accessible to look at and hold in the natural as the ultimate corporeal point of contact and an unmovable absolute truth.

Of the highest use, the Word of God is to be believed entirely; but when it is mixed with faith, there is nothing the Word of God cannot do through you!

What does mixing your faith with the Word of God look like to you?

_____

_____

FOCUS POINT

...Just as Christ also loved the church and gave Himself for her, [26] that He might sanctify and cleanse her with the washing of water by the word.

—Ephesians 5:25-26

Let's take a moment to ponder this passage. Jesus loved the Church so much that He died a brutal death and gave us His Word; and through the Word we are being washed. This is a cleansing that helps each believer in renewing their mind, will, and emotions, but also helps us through our daily lives.

What is a way that you can be proactive in using the Word to cleanse your mind?

_____

_____

_____

_____

_____

_____

_____

_____

_____

_____

_____

_____

When we mix our faith with the Word of God, all things are possible!

Take a moment right now and speak the Word over your mind. Say this prayer with me:

Thank You, Lord, for Your Word. Thank You that through Your Word, my life is cleansed. I apply my faith to the Word right now, in Jesus' name, amen.

THERE WAS NO MEDIATOR

Moses was the mediator, or the *go-between* as described in the dictionary. He would go between the Lord and the Israelites. He was the spokesperson for the Lord. There were times when Moses also interceded for the Israelites when the Lord's anger was fierce over them and Moses asked the Lord to spare their lives, to which the Lord listened several times.

Have you ever been a mediator or the go-between person? Describe the situation.

_____

_____

_____

_____

_____

_____

It can be a very wearing job. It's hard not to carry the weight of the situation when you so desperately want things to work out between the two parties. Imagine the hardship it was for Moses being that person to the grumbling and complaining Israelites!

THE TRUE MEDIATOR HAD TO COME

1. Seeing God from a sinful state without the Mediator would cause a breach of God's holiness (as explained in the section titled, Without a Mediator, Holiness Kills).

From what you have read so far in this chapter, why do you think it is so vital that we have a mediator to approach God?

_____

_____

_____

_____

_____

_____

2. It would have simply killed those who saw Him.

Why do you think Uzzah was struck down for touching the ark of God?

_____

_____

_____

_____

_____

_____

David was upset at God for doing this. Do you think you would have felt the same way? Explain your answer.

_____

_____

_____

_____

_____

_____

_____

_____

_____

PEACE AND GOODWILL BETWEEN GOD AND MAN

Thank God for Jesus! Have you accepted Jesus as your personal Savior? Write down your salvation story. If you have not accepted Jesus as your Savior, I encourage you to do so now and write down your prayer below.

_____

_____

_____

_____

_____

_____

_____

_____

_____

_____

WITHOUT JESUS, THERE IS NO PROPER ACCESS TO THE FATHER

Prophecy and hearing God as a generation is a must! The days of His roar on the mountain, though not beyond Him to do so again, is not the primary way He has chosen to speak to us. We must learn His Voice.

We need to take time to learn and recognize God's Voice. What are ways that God has spoken to you?

_____

_____

_____

_____

_____

_____

What are ways that you can develop hearing the Voice of God?

_____
_____
_____
_____
_____
_____
_____

THE DAYS OF NOAH

We know that we are living in the last days, what steps do we need to take to operate effectively in the spirit of prophecy?

_____
_____
_____
_____
_____
_____
_____
_____

When you walk in His presence, darkness will have to flee because you carry the light of God in you!
How can you walk in His presence daily?

_____
_____
_____
_____
_____
_____
_____
_____
_____

PERSONAL REFLECTION

We discussed what a mediator was, a go-between. Jesus is our Mediator between the Father and us. When Jesus died on the cross, He made a way for us to approach the throne of grace with confidence. We no longer have to be in His presence afraid or terrified. We can come to Him with confidence knowing that He loves us and hears our prayers. The Lord wants the best for you. For you to experience all the Lord has for you, you need to be saved. If you have not asked Jesus to come into your life and be Lord of your everything, then you need to take a moment and do that right now. Those who do not do this necessary step will not get to experience the God of love. They will only know Him from a distance; and on that day when they will stand before Him, there will be fear and trembling and rightly so. If you would like to give your life to Jesus, say this prayer out loud where you are:

> *Dear Jesus,*
>
> *I believe that You died on the cross to take away my sins and make a way for me to have access to the Father. I believe that You rose from the dead on the third day and defeated the grip of the devil on humanity. I ask You to come into my life and be Lord of my everything. I believe that all my sins, past, present, and future, are washed away and covered by Your blood, and to this I say, "Thank You. I love You, Lord." In Jesus' name, amen.*
>
> *If you prayed this prayer for the first time, please reach out to our office and we would like to send you a free teaching titled "Saved, Rescued for a Purpose." God bless!*

CHAPTER TWO

CONVERSATIONS IN HEAVEN

SCRIPTURES

1. **First Corinthians 13:12 KJV**— For now we see through a glass, darkly; but then face to face: now I know in part; but then shall I know even as also I am known.

2. **Ephesians 1:18 NASB1977**— I pray that the eyes of your heart may be enlightened, so that you may know what is the hope of His calling, what are the riches of the glory of His inheritance in the saints.

3. **Hebrews 12:23 NASB1977**— To the general assembly and church of the first-born who are enrolled in heaven, and to God, the Judge of all, and to the spirits of righteous men made perfect.

4. **John 10:27**— My sheep hear My voice, and I know them, and they follow Me.

5. **Jude 1:20**— But you, beloved, building yourselves up on your most holy faith, praying in the Holy Spirit.

6. **First Corinthians 14:18**— I thank my God I speak with tongues more than you all.

7. **First Corinthians 13:1**— Though I speak with the tongues of men and of angels, but have not love, I have become sounding brass or a clanging cymbal.

In all our communication and interaction, one vital thing to know is that God is always speaking. He is always speaking to you, and His great desire is to be heard and understood. Hearing God is a matter of altering you through His Word and prayer.

It might be surprising to many that God is not going to lead by speaking to your intellect! He speaks to the heart and spirit, for He is Spirit! (*See* John 4:24.)

God is always speaking; the question is are we listening? In Revelation after Jesus addresses each church, He says, *He who has ears let him hear what the Spirit is saying to the churches.* This is the key, having ears that hear His Voice.

What do you think can hinder you from having *ears to hear what the Lord is saying?*

_____

_____

_____

_____

_____

_____

_____

HEATHER'S JOURNEY TO HEAVEN

Have you ever been in an impossible situation that only a miracle would change the outcome?

_____

_____

_____

_____

_____

_____

_____

Imagine the imagery that Heather experienced, with colors that are indescribable. Have you ever thought of what your home will be like in heaven? What do you think it will look like?

_____

_____

_____

_____

_____

_____

_____

_____

HOW THE LORD SPOKE IN HEAVEN

FOCUS POINT

Thought-to-thought and heart-to-heart. When the Lord spoke, Heather knew it, and there was no doubt that the Lord was speaking to her. It resonated in her to which she responded the same way, thought-to-thought and heart-to-heart.

The Lord is always speaking, and we can still hear Him. In all times of the day. While resting, working, and in all scenarios of life, He's speaking.

God desires to speak with you daily. He desires to have fellowship with you.

> *Behold, I stand at the door and knock. If anyone hears My voice and opens the door I will come in to him and dine with him, and he with Me.*
>
> **—Revelation 3:20**

This verse shows the heart of Jesus. He's knocking on our hearts waiting for an invitation to come into our lives. He wants to dine with us. This means He wants fellowship, relationship, and He wants to speak with us. He doesn't give a timeline to how long He'll stay, that's because once He's invited in, He's here forever!

If you feel that you don't hear His Voice, like you haven't learned His Voice, take this time right now to spend time with Him. Invite Him to join you for fellowship and relationship. Pray this with me:

> *Dear Jesus, thank You that You desire to have fellowship with me. I ask that I have ears to hear what You are saying. I cancel all other noise and voices that are hindering me from knowing Your Voice. I pray that as You speak, my mind and heart will know it and there will be no confusion that would try to rob me of what You are saying. In Jesus' name, amen.*

SPOKEN WORDS ARE FALLEN

Why do you think Eve was so deceived? And why do you think Adam decided to rebel against the Lord by taking of the fruit?

_____

_____

_____

_____

What are ways that you can renew your mind?

_____

_____

_____

_____

CLEAR THE MECHANISM

Other than speaking heart-to-heart or Spirit-to-spirit, what are other ways that God speaks to His sheep?

_____

_____

_____

_____

CLARITY IS GOD'S NATIVE TONGUE

Why do you think it is so vital to speak in tongues?

_____

_____

_____

_____

Why do you think the enemy hates when Christians pray in tongues?

_____

_____

_____

_____

_____

_____

_____

_____

_____

_____

_____

PERSONAL REFLECTION

But you, beloved, building yourselves up on your most holy faith, praying in the Holy Spirit.

—Jude 1:20

The Lord desires that we all be filled with the Holy Spirit with the evidence of speaking in tongues. If you have not received this gift, take this time with the Lord, and pray the following prayer:

Dear heavenly Father,

I come to You with a desire to speak in my heavenly language. I pray that Your Holy Spirit would fill me with the evidence of speaking in tongues. I silence every thought of confusion and I pray that Your peace would guide my thoughts and my mouth would begin to speak freely and without hindrances. In Jesus' name, amen.

Now let the Holy Spirit move and as a faith act, begin to start moving your mouth and tongue. The Lord will not move your mouth, He will fill it once you start moving. Now that you have received the wonderful gift, take this time to pray before the Lord.

Praise God for His gifts and that we can use them for our good and the good of others!

CHAPTER THREE

MULTIDIMENSIONAL GOD

SCRIPTURES

1. **Exodus 33:23**— Then I will take away My hand, and you shall see My back; but My face shall not be seen.

2. **First Corinthians 13:9**— For we know in part and we prophesy in part.

3. **Ezekiel 1:15-16**— Now as I looked at the living creatures, behold, a wheel was on the earth beside each living creature with its four faces. [16] The appearance of the wheels and their workings was like the color of beryl, and all four had the same likeness. **The appearance of their workings was, as it were, a wheel in the middle of a wheel.**

4. **Ezekiel 1:9 KJV**— Their **wings were joined** one to another; they turned not when they went; they went every one straight forward.

5. **Revelation 4:6-9 KJV**— And before the throne there was a sea of glass like unto crystal: and in the midst of the throne, and round about the throne, were **four beasts** full of eyes before and behind. [7] And the first beast was like a lion, and the second beast like a calf, and the third beast had a face as a man, and the fourth beast was like a flying eagle. [8] And the four beasts had each of them six wings about him; and they were full of eyes within: and they rest not day and night, saying, Holy, holy, holy, Lord God Almighty, which was, and is, and is to come. [9] And when those beasts give glory and honor and thanks to him that sat on the throne, who liveth for ever and ever.

6. **Genesis 1:2-3 KJV**— And the earth was without form, and void; and darkness was upon the face of the deep. And the Spirit of God moved upon the face of the waters. [3] And God said, Let there be light: and there was light.

7. **Luke 9:30 KJV**— And, behold, there talked with him two men, which were Moses and Elias.

8. **Mark 9:4 KJV**— And there appeared unto them Elias with Moses: and they were talking with Jesus.

9. **Matthew 17:3 KJV**— And, behold, there appeared unto them Moses and Elias talking with him.

GOD SUPERSEDES TIME AND HISTORY

When looking at the Greek definition of "revelation," it's an amazing thing to consider that as we read the Word of God, we are *uncovering* and *revealing* the Revelation of Jesus.

How many times have you read a verse and received a revelation from it, just to read it again and get a new revelation! It's incredible that the Word of God is alive and is speaking each time we read it.

Can you think of a specific verse that you have had multiple revelations after reading it more than once? If so, write down the verse and what you received each time you read it.

_____

_____

_____

_____

_____

_____

_____

_____

_____

_____

_____

OUR INFINITE GOD

Joseph gave an illustration of a parade and how God sees the beginning from the end. How has this understanding changed the way you perceive God?

_____

_____

_____

_____

_____

_____

_____

FOCUS POINT

As we think of our God as our Infinite Father, Psalm 139 gives us glimpses into what this looks like on a personal level.

> *You have searched me, Lord, and you know me.* [2] *You know when I sit and when I rise; you perceive my thoughts from afar.* [3] *You discern my going out and my lying down; you are familiar with all my ways.* [4] *Before a word is on my tongue you, Lord, know it completely.* [5] *You hem me in behind and before, and you lay your hand upon me.* [6] *Such knowledge is too wonderful for me, too lofty for me to attain.* [7] *Where can I go from your Spirit? Where can I flee from your presence?* [8] *If I go up to the heavens, you are there; if I make my bed in the depths, you are there.* [9] *If I rise on the wings of the dawn, if I settle on the far side of the sea,* [10] *even there your hand will guide me, your right hand will hold me fast.* [11] *If I say, "Surely the darkness will hide me and the light become night around me,"* [12] *even the darkness will not be dark to you; the night will shine like the day, for darkness is as light to you.* [13] *For you created my inmost being; you knit me together in my mother's womb.* [14] *I praise you because I am fearfully and wonderfully made; your works are wonderful, I know that full well.* [15] *My frame was not hidden from you when I was made in the secret place, when I was woven together in the depths of the earth.* [16] *Your eyes saw my unformed body; all the days ordained for me were written in your book before one of them came to be.* [17] *How precious to me are your thoughts, God! How vast is the sum of them!* [18] *Were I to count them, they would outnumber the grains of sand—when I awake, I am still with you.*
>
> **—Psalm 139:1-18 NIV**

Isn't that an amazing passage of scripture verses! God knows you. He knew you before He created you in your mother's womb. The passage goes on to say, "Where can I go from your Spirit?" He is everywhere! When you feel that you are alone, He is there waiting for you to reach out to Him. Take this time to meditate on this scripture passage and allow the Holy Spirit to speak to you and pour His love on you. On the following page, write what stands out to you in this passage from God's Word.

_____

_____

_____

_____

_____

_____

_____

_____

_____

_____

_____

_____

_____

_____

_____

_____

_____

_____

EZEKIEL'S INTERDIMENSIONAL WHEEL

How do the visions of the throne of God that Ezekiel and John saw help us to understand the uniqueness of God's viewpoint of space and time?

_____

_____

_____

_____

_____

_____

Joseph explains the Hebrew word for "back"; taking into consideration the definition in Chapter Three of the book, do you think it's possible that Moses, while looking at God's back, was shown the beginning of time and this is how he was able to write Genesis 1? Write your thoughts below.

_____

_____

_____

_____

_____

_____

_____

_____

_____

_____

_____

_____

_____

_____

_____

_____

_____

_____

_____

_____

_____

_____

_____

_____

_____

_____

_____

_____

_____

PERSONAL REFLECTION

Ask, and it will be given to you; seek, and you will find; knock, and it will be opened to you. [8] *For everyone who asks receives, and he who seeks finds, and to him who knocks it will be opened.*

—Matthew 7:7-8

The Lord desires to speak to you. He wants to be sought after. The promise He gives is that those who seek Him will find Him. Those who knock, He will open the door. Take this time to seek Him and spend time with Him. As you do, pray the following prayer:

Dear heavenly Father,

I come to You today, Lord, with a heart that wants to seek You until I find You. Reveal Yourself to me in a new way. I desire to have fellowship with You. You are welcome in this place, I draw near to You, Lord, and I thank You that You are drawing near to me. I welcome all the gifts that are offered in Your Word. In Jesus' name, amen.

Take time right now to write down anything the Lord spoke to you in this time of personal reflection.

_____

_____

_____

_____

_____

_____

_____

_____

_____

_____

_____

_____

_____

_____

_____

_____

CHAPTER FOUR

THE PROPHETIC SPECTRUM

THE FOUR TYPES OF PROPHECY

SCRIPTURES

1. **First Samuel 9:9**— Formerly in Israel, when a man went to inquire of God, he spoke thus: "Come, let us go to the seer"; for he who is now called a prophet was formerly called a seer.

2. **First Corinthians 9:1-2**— Am I not an apostle? Am I not free? Have I not seen Jesus Christ our Lord? Are you not my work in the Lord? [2] **If I am not an apostle to others, yet doubtless I am to you.** For you are the seal of my apostleship in the Lord.

3. **Ephesians 4:11-12**— And He Himself gave some to be apostles, some prophets, some evangelists, and some pastors and teachers, [12] **for the equipping of the saints** for the work of ministry, **for the edifying of the body of Christ.**

4. **First Corinthians 14:3**— But he who prophesies speaks **edification** and **exhortation** and **comfort** to men.

5. **First Corinthians 12:8**— For to one is given the word of wisdom through the Spirit, to another the **word of knowledge** through the same Spirit.

6. **First Corinthians 14:24**— But **if all prophesy**, and an unbeliever or an uninformed person comes in, he is convinced by all, he is convicted by all.

7. **First Corinthians 1:26-29**— For you see your calling, brethren, that not many wise according to the flesh, not many mighty, not many noble, are called. [27] But God has chosen the foolish things of the world to put to shame the wise, and God has chosen the weak things of the world to put to shame the things which are mighty; [28] and the base things of the world and the things which are despised God has chosen, and the things which are not, to bring to nothing the things that are, [29] that no flesh should glory in His presence.

8. **Romans 12:6**— Having then gifts differing according to the grace that is given to us, let us use them: if prophecy, let us prophesy in proportion to our faith.

9. **Acts 15:32**— Now Judas and Silas, themselves being prophets also, exhorted and strengthened the brethren with many words.

10. **James 1:17**— Every good gift and every perfect gift is from above, and comes down from the Father of lights, with whom there is no variation or shadow of turning.

11. **First Chronicles 29:29**— Now the acts of David the king, first and last, behold, they are written in the book of Samuel the **seer**, and in the book of Nathan the **prophet**, and in the book of Gad the **seer.**

12. **Psalm 17:15 NASB1977**— As for me, **I shall behold** Thy face in righteousness; I will be satisfied with Thy likeness when I awake.

13. **Isaiah 47:13**— You are wearied in the multitude of your counsels; let now the astrologers, the **stargazers**, and the monthly prognosticators stand up and save you from what shall come upon you.

14. **Lamentations 2:14**— Your prophets have **seen** for you false and deceptive visions; they have not uncovered your iniquity, to bring back your captives, but have envisioned for you false prophecies and delusions.

15. **Ezekiel 12:27**— Son of man, look, the house of Israel is saying, "The **vision** that he sees is for many days from now, and he prophesies of times far off."

16. **Habakkuk 1:1**— The burden which the prophet Habakkuk **saw.**

17. **Zechariah 10:2**— For the idols speak delusion; the diviners **envision** lies and tell false dreams; they comfort in vain. Therefore, the people wend their way like sheep; they are in trouble because there is no shepherd.

18. **Second Kings 8:10-12**— And Elisha said to him, "Go, say to him, 'You shall certainly recover.' However, the Lord has shown me that he will really die." [11] Then **he set his countenance in a stare until he was ashamed; and the man of God wept.** [12] And Hazael said, "Why is my lord weeping?" He answered, "Because I know the evil that you will do to the children of Israel: Their strongholds you will set on fire, and their young men you will kill with the sword; and you will dash their children and rip open their women with child.

19. **Second Kings 8:14-15**— Then he departed from Elisha, and came to his master, who said to him, "What did Elisha say to you?" And he answered, "He told me you would surely recover." [15] But it happened on the next day that he took a thick cloth and dipped it in water, and spread it over his face so that he died; and Hazael reigned in his place.

20. **Second Corinthians 12:1-4**— It is doubtless not profitable for me to boast. I will come to visions and revelations of the Lord: [2] I know a man in Christ who fourteen years ago—**whether in the body I do not know, or whether out of the body I do not know**, God knows—such a one was caught up to the third heaven. [3] And I know such a man—**whether in the body or out of the body**

I do not know, God knows—[4] how he was caught up into Paradise and heard inexpressible words, which it is not lawful for a man to utter.

21. **Daniel 9:24**— Seventy weeks are determined for your people and for your holy city, to finish the transgression, to make an end of sins, to make reconciliation for iniquity, to bring in everlasting righteousness, to seal up **vision** and prophecy, and to anoint the Most Holy.

22. **Daniel 10:14**— Now I have come to make you understand what will happen to your people in the latter days, for the **vision** refers to many days yet to come.

23. **Psalm 17:15**— As for me, I will **see** Your face in righteousness; I shall be satisfied when I awake in Your likeness.

24. **Isaiah 47:13**— You are wearied in the multitude of your counsels; let now the astrologers, the stargazers, and the monthly prognosticators stand up and save you from what shall come upon you.

25. **Isaiah 1:1**— The vision of Isaiah the son of Amoz, which he saw concerning Judah and Jerusalem in the days of Uzziah, Jotham, Ahaz, and Hezekiah, kings of Judah.

26. **Revelation 1:1-2**— The **Revelation** of Jesus Christ, which God gave Him to show His servants— things which must shortly take place. And He sent and signified it by His angel to His servant John, [2] who bore witness to the word of God, and to the testimony of Jesus Christ, to all things that he saw.

What is the distinction between the office of the prophet and the gift of prophecy?

_____

_____

_____

_____

_____

_____

_____

_____

_____

_____

_____

_____

_____

PAUL WAS THEIR APOSTLE

To help us understand the fivefold ministry, Paul gives a breakdown of each governmental office and then a job description. Why is it important for believers to know these offices, their operations, and purpose?

_____

_____

_____

_____

_____

_____

_____

_____

_____

_____

A PROPHET'S JURISDICTION

Prophets have a responsibility to those who recognize them as a prophet because God graced them for that segment of the body.

Do you personally know a prophet who is assigned to your local church body? What was it that distinguished this person as a prophet in your area?

_____

_____

_____

_____

_____

_____

_____

_____

_____

_____

GLARING WORD OF KNOWLEDGE BY ALL

In what way does the fourth operation of prophecy complete the classical understanding of the ways prophecy functions within the Church?

_____

_____

_____

_____

_____

_____

_____

An uninformed person, by the very nature of the label _uniformed_, means one who has no prior understanding regarding what is happening in the type of church they are walking into. How does a corporate word of knowledge impact the uninformed person?

_____

_____

_____

_____

_____

_____

_____

_____

List the two reasons why God uses His body of believers in magnificent ways concerning the realm of the prophetic.

1. _____

_____

_____

_____

2. _____

_____

_____

_____

FOCUS POINT

Have you ever received a word of knowledge from someone? If so, what was it and did it minister to you in a special way?

_____

_____

_____

_____

_____

_____

_____

_____

_____

_____

_____

_____

_____

_____

_____

_____

_____

_____

_____

_____

_____

_____

_____

Take this time to think about what you wrote down and spend time with the Lord reflecting on His goodness in using someone to minister to you.

GOVERNING MINISTRY OFFICE—NOT A HIERARCHY

When someone is called to the office of the prophet, what should their ministry encompass?

_____

_____

_____

_____

_____

_____

_____

_____

THE PROPHETIC SPECTRUM

The following are the four different types of prophecy; for each one, write what stood out to you in each type.

1. Roeh – The Visionary Seer, Mobilizer Prophet

_____

_____

_____

_____

_____

_____

_____

_____

2. Nabi – The Proclaiming Prophet

_____

_____

_____

_____

_____

_____

_____

3. Chazah – The Gazing Prophet

_____

_____

_____

_____

_____

_____

_____

4. Chozeh (Hebrew) – A Beholder; one who leans forward, peering into the distance.

_____

_____

_____

_____

_____

_____

_____

Joseph concluded the chapter by saying, "You do not have to attempt to move in any of the operations of the prophetic, pray in the Spirit, read your Bible, or get to know God! The gifts will find you!"

PERSONAL REFLECTION

Pursue love, and desire spiritual gifts, but especially that you may prophesy.

—1 Corinthians 14:1

In 1 Corinthians 14:1, it says to desire spiritual gifts. Everything that we find in the Scriptures is a message from the Lord to us. We can stand on the promises of the Word. When it says to desire spiritual gifts, that means these gifts are for you and me. Take this time to seek the Lord in His Word and start declaring the truth of His Word over your life.

Dear Lord,

I thank You that Your Word says we should pursue love and desire spiritual gifts. I desire all the gifts that You offer to me through Your Holy Spirit. I desire the gift of prophecy. Lord, use me to not only pursue love but to show love to those around me through the gifts that You freely offer. Thank You for all that You have given me and all that is coming as I seek You in Your Word. In Jesus' name, amen.

Take time right now to write down anything the Lord spoke to you in this time of personal reflection.

_____

_____

_____

_____

_____

_____

_____

_____

_____

_____

_____

_____

_____

_____

_____

CHAPTER FIVE

PROPHETIC DNA—WITCHCRAFT OR LEGITIMATE?

SCRIPTURES

1. **Amos 7:14-15**— Then Amos answered and said to Amaziah: "I was no prophet, **nor was I a son of a prophet**, but I was a sheepbreeder and a tender of sycamore fruit. [15] Then the Lord took me as I followed the flock, and the Lord said to me, 'Go, prophesy to My people Israel.'"

2. **First Samuel 3:4-7**— That the Lord called Samuel. And he answered, "Here I am!" [5] So he ran to Eli and said, "Here I am, for you called me." And he said, "I did not call; lie down again." And he went and lay down. [6] Then the Lord called yet again, "Samuel!" So Samuel arose and went to Eli, and said, "Here I am, for you called me." He answered, "I did not call, my son; lie down again." [7] (Now Samuel did not yet know the Lord, nor was the word of the Lord yet revealed to him.)

3. **Second Timothy 1:5**— When I call to remembrance the genuine faith that is in you, which **dwelt first in your grandmother Lois and your mother Eunice, and I am persuaded is in you also.**

4. **Acts 21:7-10**— And when we had finished our voyage from Tyre, we came to Ptolemais, greeted the brethren, and stayed with them one day. [8] On the next day we who were Paul's companions departed and came to Caesarea, and entered the house of Philip the evangelist, who was one of the seven, and stayed with him. [9] **Now this man had four virgin daughters who prophesied.** [10] And as we stayed many days, a certain prophet named Agabus came down from Judea.

Can a prophetic gifting be inherited? Where do we find this in the Bible?

_____

_____

_____

_____

_____

_____

_____

NORMALCY BIAS

Joseph describes *normalcy bias* as when "something strange and out of place occurs, but everyone subconsciously ignores it and goes on with life as usual." Can you think of something in your life that normalcy bias has become the result?

_____

_____

_____

_____

_____

_____

HOW PSYCHICS ARE MADE

How are psychics "made," and what is the deception they believe?

_____

_____

_____

_____

_____

_____

SPIRITUAL DNA

Why is a relationship with Jesus so important in avoiding deception?

_____

_____

_____

_____

_____

_____

GIFTS MISHANDLED IN THE CHURCH

If a "new-to-gifts" person is mishandled by the church they attend, what can educated believers do to help that person?

_____

_____

_____

_____

_____

_____

WHAT SPIRIT IS DRIVING THE GIFT

As believers, how do we discern the spirit behind the gift that is manifesting in an individual?

_____

_____

_____

_____

_____

PERSONAL REFLECTION

Your life matters: a high act of worship to the Lord is when we surrender all we are and have to Him!

> _But the hour is coming, and now is, when the true worshipers will worship the Father in spirit and truth; for the Father is seeking such to worship Him._
>
> **—John 4:23**

We know that the Holy Spirit is the One who awakens us to the understanding of who God is. We also know that Jesus is the way, the _truth_, and the life (John 14:6). Through Jesus and the Holy Spirit, we can worship the Lord. Why? Because He is seeking people who know who Jesus is and who have the Holy Spirit living inside them. As you spend time with Jesus meditating on what the John 4:23 means to you, take this time to invite the Holy Spirit to show you what this type of worship is and how you can walk in it.

Dear Lord,

I invite Your Holy Spirit to come and show me how to worship in Spirit and in truth. Reveal to me through Your Word who You are and how to walk out John 4:23. Thank You for pouring Your love and Spirit over me, in Jesus' name. Amen.

Take time right now to write down anything the Lord spoke to you in this time of personal reflection.

_____

_____

_____

_____

_____

_____

_____

_____

_____

_____

_____

_____

_____

_____

_____

_____

_____

_____

_____

_____

_____

CHAPTER SIX

ENCOUNTERS WITH THE SPIRIT

SCRIPTURES

1. **Revelation 4:1**— Come up here, and I will show you things which must take place after this.

2. **Matthew 16:24-25**— If anyone desires to come after Me, let him deny himself, and take up his cross, and follow Me. [25] For whoever desires to save his life will lose it, but whoever loses his life for My sake will find it.

How important is the written Word of God to those who are experiencing encounters with the Spirit? What are the ways the Word of God impacts your life?

_____

_____

_____

_____

_____

_____

_____

_____

_____

MY NAME ON A WHITE STONE

Joseph's name was written, by nature, on a stone. This was a God moment, teaching him to know and trust God's Voice. A confirmation that he heard right.

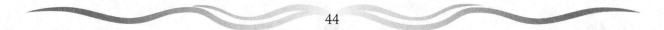

Have you had a moment of confirmation from the Lord as you were learning to recognize His Voice? If so, explain.

_____

_____

_____

_____

_____

DEALING WITH WITCHCRAFT

Some examples of witchcraft and encountering witchcraft and the demonic were given in this chapter. Have you ever experienced encounters with witchcraft or with someone manifesting demonic behavior? What have you learned from these chapters so far that could have helped you to deal with the situation perhaps in a more biblically grounded way?

_____

_____

_____

_____

_____

CALLING ON ANGELS

In Joseph's book *Servants of Fire*, he addresses how angels only respond to the Voice of God. He continues on by saying that angel's respond to the Voice of God through believers. The following is a portion taken out of Chapter Four, "The Secret of Voice Activation."

> Angels are moved to *serve the heirs of salvation*. They receive kingdom access and permission from believers who speak the Word of God, who God mixed with their faith. There is compliance with God's way of doing things, which produces covenant empowerment.
>
> When we pray in faith, there isn't necessarily the commanding of angels—they simply know what to do. Meaning, when you take your free moral agency and begin to pray in the

Holy Spirit, prayers of faith will engage the authority of God and engage the authority of man, who is a little lower than God according to Psalm 8:5. A combination of man's free moral agency and rank among all created beings offers the authority to pray and authorize angels as well. Again, it should be stated that we are not commanding these fiery servants. Rather, how we pray and the way we engage in warfare prayer brings about kingdom effectiveness.

Servants of Fire, page 86

Have you had a time when you know angels intervened in a difficult or dangerous situation? If so, write what happened.

_____
_____
_____
_____
_____
_____
_____
_____
_____
_____
_____
_____
_____
_____
_____
_____
_____
_____
_____
_____

A SUPERNATURAL KNOWING

FOCUS POINT

Have you encountered someone who displays false humility? Have you ever noticed it in yourself, even for a moment? Take time to discover what false humility is and how you can protect yourself from it. First and Second Timothy are excellent sources for learning more about false humility. Below is space for you to write down what revelation you receive after reading First and Second Timothy.

_____

_____

_____

_____

_____

_____

_____

_____

_____

_____

_____

_____

_____

_____

_____

_____

_____

_____

_____

_____

_____

Take this time to think about what you wrote down and spend time with the Lord reflecting on His goodness in using someone to minister to you.

THE DISCOVERY OF AUTHORITY

Many people are unwilling to *"give up to go up."* Meaning that they are not willing to follow Jesus, no matter the cost. When you truly surrender all to Him, you enter a position of absolute authority.

In Matthew 16:24-25, Jesus says, "If anyone desires to come after Me, let him deny himself, and take up his cross, and follow Me. [25] For whoever desires to save his life will lose it, but whoever loses his life for My sake will find it."

This is what *"giving up to go up"* means: if you lose your life by exchanging it for the life of Jesus, you will actually gain everything you never knew you wanted! There is a higher way to live, and it is found in the truth of the Gospel. When you discover it, it will make you bold!

PERSONAL REFLECTION

Finding your authority in Jesus is a powerful realization! When did you first discover you had authority in Him? If you haven't yet experienced standing in your authority as a son or daughter of the Most High King, consider that Jesus said we must give up our lives to follow Him. That means total surrender! If you haven't fully surrendered to Him, take time now to write a prayer of submission to Him. You'll be amazed at what happens next!

Take time right now to write down anything the Lord spoke to you in this time of personal reflection.

_____

_____

_____

_____

_____

_____

_____

_____

_____

_____

_____

_____

_____

_____

SECTION TWO

NAVIGATING AND INTERPRETING THE SPIRIT REALM

CHAPTER SEVEN

THE MAP AND THE TERRITORY

SCRIPTURES

1. **First Corinthians 13:9**— For we know in part and we prophesy in part.

2. **John 6:63**— It is the Spirit who gives life; the flesh profits nothing. The words that I speak to you are spirit, and they are life.

3. **Acts 15:28**—For it seemed good to the Holy Spirit, and to us, to lay upon you no greater burden than these necessary things.

4. **Proverbs 20:27 KJV**— The spirit of man is the candle of the Lord, searching all the inward parts of the belly.

5. **Hebrews 5:14**— But solid food belongs to those who are of full age, that is, those who by reason of use have their senses exercised to discern both good and evil.

6. **Romans 12:2**— And do not be conformed to this world, but be transformed by the renewing of your mind, that you may prove what is that good and acceptable and perfect will of God.

7. **First Thessalonians 5:20**— Do not despise prophecies.

8. **James 4:6**— But He gives more grace. Therefore He says: "God resists the proud, but gives grace to the humble."

9. **Hebrews 10:22**— Let us draw near with a true heart in full assurance of faith, having our hearts sprinkled from an evil conscience and our bodies washed with pure water.

10. **First Corinthians 14:1**— Pursue love, and **desire spiritual gifts**, but **especially that you may prophesy**.

How has the principle of "the map and the territory" helped you to understand more fully what prophetic encounters are and how to navigate them?

_____

_____

_____

_____

What is a sensory compass and what must it be grounded on in order for a person to appropriately apply it to real-world situations?

_____

_____

_____

_____

FOCUS POINT

Of great importance is the recognition that no one has everything perfected, yet we are to pursue clarity and sharpen our walk of faith constantly. The Spirit is perfect, and we are to continuously place ourselves in the Word of God to walk in that perfection accurately. Take this time and ask the Holy Spirit to examine your life and reveal to you anything that needs to be sharpened in your life.

_____

_____

_____

_____

_____

_____

Take this time to think about what you wrote down; and as He reveals things to you, ask Him to give you creative ideas of how to sharpen these areas and bring clarity.

INTERPRETING PROPHETIC HAPPENINGS

Heuristic

Why is it acceptable for a person who has a heart full of the Word of God and faith, to interpret a prophetic moment using the heuristic method?

_____

_____

_____

_____

_____

RIGHTSIZING THE PROPHETIC MANIA

As discussed in this chapter, many strange things happen in the prophetic community. How do we discern what is true and of the Lord, as well as help those developing their gifts to have a firm foundation?

_____

_____

_____

_____

_____

ENAMORED WITH PROPHETS

How do people fall into the wandering loop of voices?

_____

_____

_____

_____

_____

Why does God allow us to know in part, prophesy in part, and see through a glass dimly?

_____

_____

_____

_____

_____

_____

_____

THE POWER OF HUMILITY

How do we use the power of humility to navigate the gifts of prophecy?

_____

_____

_____

_____

_____

_____

USE REASON

What makes someone a candidate to have their "fledgling emotions and untrained discernment" taken advantage of?

_____

_____

_____

_____

_____

_____

_____

NEVER FOLLOW A SECOND LIEUTENANT

What is the lesson of not following the second lieutenant?

_____

_____

_____

_____

NEW TIMES, SAME HOLY SPIRIT

What makes someone a disciple of Jesus Christ?

_____

_____

_____

_____

NAVIGATING THE DESIRE TO PROPHESY

*Pursue love, and **desire spiritual gifts, but especially that you may prophesy.***

—1 Corinthians 14:1

Consider the definition of "desire" and explain a better way to say 1 Corinthians 14:1. How can you apply this to your life?

_____

_____

_____

_____

_____

_____

_____

_____

_____

ARE YOU TRAINED OR UNTRAINED

Just like an athlete needs to train their skill or gift, the body of Christ should be training our spiritual gifts. What are ways you can train and develop the gift of prophecy?

_____

_____

_____

_____

TRUE NORTH

If someone has a compass and understands its use, they will be able to navigate through any terrain and go anywhere. When we understand that hearing the Lord is our spiritual compass, we will be able to make it through all things that come our way, both in the prophetic and all areas of our lives.

SHARPENED CLARITY

What are ways that you can develop discernment using your senses, and how can this help you recognize good versus evil?

_____

_____

_____

_____

PROPHETIC VOLTAGE AND DISCERNMENT

In what ways can offense and hardship come into the life of a prophetic person?

_____

_____

_____

_____

PERSONAL REFLECTION

Examine the tools God gives us to navigate the desire to prophesy. What stands out to you as important keys to know in developing this gift and how can you apply it to yourself?

Take time right now to write down anything the Lord spoke to you in this time of personal reflection.

_____

_____

_____

_____

_____

_____

_____

_____

_____

_____

_____

_____

_____

_____

_____

_____

_____

_____

_____

_____

_____

CHAPTER EIGHT

A BETTER HERMENEUTIC
REVELATION, INTERPRETATION, APPLICATION

SCRIPTURES

1. **First Corinthians 4:6 NIV** — So that you may learn from us the meaning of the saying, "Do not go beyond what is written." Then you will not be puffed up in being a follower of one of us over against the other.

2. **Proverbs 29:18** — Where there is no revelation, the people cast off restraint; but happy is he who keeps the law.

3. **First Thessalonians 5:23** — Now may the God of peace Himself sanctify you completely; and may your whole **spirit, soul,** and **body** be preserved blameless at the coming of our Lord Jesus Christ.

4. **Hebrews 12:23** — To the general assembly and church of the firstborn who are registered in heaven, to God the Judge of all, **to the spirits of just men made perfect.**

5. **Romans 12:2** — And do not be conformed to this world, but be transformed by the **renewing of your mind,** that you may prove what is that good and acceptable and perfect will of God.

6. **Hebrews 5:14 KJV** — But strong meat belongeth to them that are of full age, even those who by reason of use have their **senses exercised to discern** both good and evil.

7. **John 6:63** — It is the Spirit who gives life; the flesh profits nothing. **The words that I speak to you are spirit,** and they are life.

8. **Revelation 19:10** — The testimony of Jesus is the spirit of prophecy.

9. **John 1:1** — In the beginning was the Word, and the Word was with God, and the Word was God.

10. **James 1:8** — He is a **double-minded man,** unstable in all his ways.

11. **James 1:23-24**— For if anyone is a hearer of the word and not a doer, he **is like a man observing his natural face in a mirror; 24 for he observes himself, goes away, and immediately forgets what kind of man he was.**

12. **Acts 15:28**— For **it seemed good** to the **Holy Spirit, and to us…**

13. **Matthew 16:15-17**— He said to them, "But who do you say that I am?" [16] Simon Peter answered and said, "You are the Christ, the Son of the living God." [17] Jesus answered and said to him, "Blessed are you, Simon Bar-Jonah, for flesh and blood has not revealed this to you, but My Father who is in heaven."

14. **John 1:48**— Nathanael said to Him, "How do You know me?" Jesus answered and said to him, "Before Philip called you, when you were under the fig tree, I saw you."

15. **John 4:19**— The woman said to Him, "Sir, I perceive that You are a prophet."

16. **John 4:29**— "Come, see a Man who told me all things that I ever did. Could this be the Christ?"

17. **Second Peter 1:19-21**— And so we have the prophetic word confirmed, which you do well to heed as a light that shines in a dark place, until the day dawns and the morning star rises in your hearts; knowing this first, that no prophecy of Scripture is of any private interpretation, for prophecy never came by the will of man, but holy men of God spoke as they were moved by the Holy Spirit.

In this chapter, we discuss the process of revelation, interpretation, and application. It is critical that this process is utilized to discern the prophetic message being given and its appropriate application.

NOT HITTING THE MARK

How does disappointment and confusion cause disillusionment with spiritual gifts when a prophetic word keeps missing the mark?

_____

_____

_____

_____

_____

_____

_____

_____

THE BIAS LENS

When hearing a prophetic word, it is very important to take several things into consideration, such as, the person delivering the prophetic word, their biased lens, doctrinal cloud, or opinions. Explain why this is so important when receiving a word for yourself.

_____

_____

_____

_____

_____

_____

_____

_____

TAKE THE HEART OF A WORD

Joseph explains that he usually shares about 20 to 40 percent of what he sees. Using discernment when releasing a word to someone is vital. If something is unclear, it is better to not say anything than to add your thoughts to the word, unless led to do so by the Holy Spirit.

List a few reasons why it could be dangerous to add to a prophetic word and why it is so vital to use wisdom and discernment when releasing a word.

_____

_____

_____

_____

_____

_____

_____

SPECULATION INTRODUCES CONFUSION

True prophetic ministry is to get the heart of an issue across to the recipients because God is a "heart God."

The Oxford Languages Dictionary defines "speculation" as *the forming of a theory or conjecture without firm evidence.* How can speculating bring confusion to someone when receiving or releasing a prophecy?

_____

_____

_____

_____

_____

_____

_____

_____

FOCUS POINT

You can't say the right thing to the wrong people, and you can never seem to say the wrong thing to the right people. Have you ever been around someone that everything you say is the wrong thing? Being in the presence of someone who is like this can be very discouraging. It is very important to surround yourself with like-minded people. Those who are the "right" people in your life.

Take this time to examine yourself. What would you consider yourself to be, the "right" person or the "wrong" person? Depending on your answer, explain the process that you can take to be the "right" person for those around you. Write down whatever the Holy Spirit reveals to you about yourself in this area. Be honest and let Him minister to you in this time.

_____

_____

_____

_____

_____

_____

_____

_____

_____

_____

_____

_____

_____

_____

REVELATION, INTERPRETATION, APPLICATION

First Thessalonians 5:23 lists three parts that make up a person. Joseph uses these three parts to develop the biblical process that he labeled revelation, interpretation, and application. List the three parts that make up a person and explain each part.

_____

_____

_____

_____

_____

_____

_____

_____

Revelation

Spirit - Revelation

Revelation is revealed knowledge to your spirit man! A revelation can also be a "lightbulb" moment. The Lord uses many ways to give a revelation to someone. Take a moment to think about the last revelation that you received. Was it from someone directly or the Holy Spirit speaking to you? Share the revelation you received and what you have done with that revelation?

_____

_____

_____

_____

_____

_____

Revelation Needs Scripture

What causes people who receive a revelation to go off and do something presumptuously without giving it another thought?

_____

_____

_____

_____

_____

_____

A Revelation Alone Is Not Enough

Why do you think so many in the Church are going from revelation to revelation and experience to experience?

_____

_____

_____

_____

_____

_____

Discipline Must Be Applied to Your Revelation

*For if anyone is a hearer of the word and not a doer, he **is like a man observing his natural face in a mirror;** [24] for **he observes himself, goes away, and immediately forgets what kind of man he was.***

—James 1:23-24

How does a double-minded man lose his revelation once he leaves the place where he received that word?

_____

_____

_____

_____

_____

_____

_____

_____

A revelation needs to be cultivated by what two things so that a revelation won't be lost or forgotten?

_____

_____

_____

_____

_____

_____

_____

_____

_____

Interpretation

Soul - Interpretation

*For **it seemed good** to the **Holy Spirit, and to us**....*

—Acts 15:28

Interpretation is the process of extracting the heart, intent, and meaning of what God said.

Why is it so vital to interpret a word with the help of the Holy Spirit and the guidance of godly counsel?

_____
_____
_____
_____
_____
_____
_____

Misinterpreting a Revelation

The illustration about the man misinterpreting the word "Africa" by going to Africa instead of supporting a missionary from Africa caused hardship for him. Have you ever been in a situation where you misinterpreted a word and learned a hard lesson? If so, write about it here.

_____
_____
_____
_____
_____
_____
_____
_____

Revealed by the Spirit

List some examples in the Bible where the Spirit revealed what the revelation was and helped the individual interpret correctly?

_____
_____
_____
_____
_____
_____
_____

Application

Natural/Body - Application

The Necessary Attribute of Peace

Application is where we act in faith on what we heard. Why is peace a necessary attribute of application of a prophetic word spoken over you?

_____

_____

_____

_____

_____

_____

_____

New Traditions about Prophecy

Some say that "God will never tell you something you didn't already know yourself." Joseph brings up the story of Naaman, in 2 Kings 5. How does this chapter debunk that saying? How does a new word induce faith and action to the hearer?

_____

_____

_____

_____

_____

_____

_____

A BETTER HERMENEUTIC

Hermeneutics—the Art and Science of Interpretation

Hermeneutics is a method of analysis through which we uncover the interpretation of a text within its context.

Prophecy Will Never Be an Exact Science

How can hermeneutics help prophetic people navigate their experiences and produce the highest and best result?

_____

_____

_____

_____

_____

_____

_____

_____

_____

_____

IF YOU DO THE DIFFICULT, GOD WILL DO THE IMPOSSIBLE!

Patience is necessary in moments of incredible breakthroughs. An accurate way of defining patience is to remain the same through all situations. To remain the same in the highs and lows. This requires discipline. How does remaining "the same" show that it matters more to you that you are doing what God desires than what you desire?

_____

_____

_____

_____

_____

_____

_____

_____

_____

_____

JUST BECAUSE YOU CAN
DOESN'T MEAN YOU SHOULD

Just as Jesus was "about His Father's business," how does this apply to the prophetic?

_____

_____

_____

_____

_____

_____

_____

_____

_____

PROPHECY NEEDS A BETTER HERMENEUTIC

In light of our discussion on hermeneutics, in what ways can prophetic people improve their practice? What are the critical concepts that are key to ensuring they are walking with the Holy Spirit in their experiences?

_____

_____

_____

_____

_____

_____

_____

_____

_____

PERSONAL REFLECTION

Revelation, interpretation, and application are the three steps that should be in place when giving or receiving a word. The Lord desires to speak to you and through you. Take this time to let the Lord examine your heart and see if you have these steps in place to not only receive a word but also so you can deliver a word to those around you.

Take time right now to write down anything the Lord spoke to you in this time of personal reflection.

_____

_____

_____

_____

_____

_____

_____

_____

_____

_____

_____

_____

_____

_____

_____

_____

_____

_____

_____

_____

CHAPTER NINE

TWO PROPHECIES, ONE KING

SCRIPTURES

1. **First Corinthians 2:14**— But the natural man does not receive the things of the Spirit of God, for they are foolishness to him; nor can he know them, because they are spiritually discerned.

2. **Ezekiel 12:13 KJV**— My net also will I spread upon him, and he shall be taken in my snare: and I will bring him to Babylon to the land of the Chaldeans; **yet shall he not see it**, though he shall die there.

3. **Jeremiah 34:3 KJV**— And thou shalt not escape out of his hand, but shalt surely be taken, and delivered into his hand; **and thine eyes shall behold the eyes of the king of Babylon**, and he shall speak with thee mouth to mouth, and thou shalt go to Babylon.

4. **Second Kings 25:5-7 KJV**— And the army of the Chaldees pursued after the king, and overtook him in the plains of Jericho: and all his army were scattered from him. [6] So they took the king and **brought him up to the king of Babylon** to Riblah; and they gave judgment upon him. [7] And they slew the sons of Zedekiah before his eyes, **and put out the eyes of Zedekiah**, and bound him with fetters of brass, and carried him to Babylon.

5. **Isaiah 9:6-7 KJV**— For unto us a child is born, unto us a son is given: and the government shall be upon his shoulder: and his name shall be called Wonderful, Counsellor, The mighty God, The everlasting Father, The Prince of Peace. [7] Of the increase of his government and peace there shall be no end, upon the throne of David, and upon his kingdom, to order it, and to establish it with judgment and with justice from henceforth even forever. The zeal of the Lord of hosts will perform this.

6. **Genesis 49:10 KJV**— The **scepter** shall not depart from Judah, nor a lawgiver from between his feet, until **Shiloh** come; and unto him shall the gathering of the people be.

7. **Daniel 9:25**— Know therefore and understand, that from the going forth of the command to restore and build Jerusalem until Messiah the Prince, there shall be seven weeks and sixty-two weeks; the street shall be built again, and the wall, even in troublesome times.

8. **Acts 21:11 KJV**— And when he was come unto us, he took Paul's girdle, and bound his own hands and feet, and said, Thus saith the Holy Ghost, **So shall the Jews at Jerusalem bind the man that owneth this girdle**, and shall deliver him into the hands of the Gentiles.

9. **Acts 21:33**— Then **the commander** came near and took him, and **commanded him to be bound** with two chains; and he asked who he was and what he had done.

10. **Acts 15:28**— For it seemed good to the Holy Spirit, and to us, to lay upon you no greater burden than these necessary things.

11. **Second Thessalonians 3:2 KJV**— And that we may be delivered from unreasonable and wicked men: for all men have not faith.

PROPHETIC VANTAGE POINTS

Vantages are interesting to consider, especially when it comes to the topic of contradictory prophetic words manifesting from two or more different sources.

Have you experienced contradictory prophecies? If so, what were they?

_____

_____

_____

_____

_____

_____

_____

EZEKIEL AND JEREMIAH'S CONFLICTING PROPHETIC WORDS

How did the two prophecies conflict with each other?

_____

_____

_____

_____

_____

_____

_____

BOTH PROPHECIES WERE FULFILLED!

As we see, both prophecies were fulfilled! Sometimes it's easy to jump to conclusion and dismiss prophetic words when they seem inaccurate. What needs to be noted is the whole picture. This is a matter of perspective or vantage point and having the full context of a matter.

THE TAKEAWAY

What is the powerful lesson learned from the prophetic words given to King Zedekiah by Ezekiel and Jeremiah the prophets?

_____

_____

_____

_____

_____

_____

_____

_____

_____

_____

_____

_____

_____

_____

_____

_____

_____

_____

_____

_____

_____

_____

FOCUS POINT

When finding the "heart of the matter" of conflicting prophetic words, why is applying patience and faith an important key to understanding a prophetic word? If this is something that you struggle with, ask the Holy Spirit to help you to walk this out. Write whatever you feel the Holy Spirit is speaking to you.

_____

_____

_____

_____

_____

_____

_____

_____

_____

_____

_____

_____

_____

_____

_____

_____

_____

CLARITY IS ALWAYS BEST

When giving a prophetic word, only say what you see. Anything added based on your interpretation of what you see might be dishonest and cause the listener much hardship.

SANHEDRIN MISINTERPRETED A PROPHECY!

What caused the Sanhedrin to misinterpret the prophecy about the Messiah?

_____
_____
_____
_____
_____

HISTORY DIFFERED
FROM THEIR INTERPRETATION

How did the Sanhedrin's misinterpretation of Messianic prophecy lead them to lose their judicial authority over the Jewish people?

_____
_____
_____
_____
_____

INTERPRETING AGABUS

Why is it important to receive the heart of the prophecy, especially in the New Testament?

_____
_____
_____
_____
_____

WAS AGABUS A FALSE PROPHET?

We know that the Lord speaks through prophetic words. These can be words of encouragement and words of warning. Agabus was not a false prophet. His word could have gotten the church to intercede on Paul's behalf and change the course of the word.

Have you been part of a scenario like this? One where the prophetic word changed because you or others were interceding? If so, write down what happened.

_____

_____

_____

_____

_____

_____

PERSONAL REFLECTION

Why is proper interpretation critical when navigating prophetic encounters? Is there a time in your own life when a prophetic word was given to you and there was confusion about the message? How did you resolve the confusion; or did misinterpretation of the message lead to circumstances that became a life lesson the Lord used to further your understanding?

_____

_____

_____

_____

_____

_____

_____

_____

_____

_____

_____

CHAPTER TEN

SENSUS PLENIOR

DEEPER FULLER MEANING

SCRIPTURES

1. **Ecclesiastes 1:9-10**— That which has been is what will be, that which is done is what will be done, and there is nothing new under the sun. [10] Is there anything of which it may be said, "See, this is new"? It has already been in ancient times before us.

2. **First Corinthians 4:6**— Now these things, brethren, I have figuratively transferred to myself and Apollos for your sakes, **that you may learn in us not to think beyond what is written,** that none of you may be puffed up on behalf of one against the other.

3. **Exodus 12:3-14**— …On the tenth of this month **every man shall take for himself a lamb,** according to the house of his father, a lamb for a household. [4] And if the household is too small for the lamb, let him and his neighbor next to his house take it according to the number of the persons; according to each man's need you shall make your count for the lamb. [5] **Your lamb shall be without blemish,** a male of the first year. You may take it from the sheep or from the goats. [6] Now you shall keep it until the fourteenth day of the same month. Then the whole assembly of the congregation of Israel shall kill it at twilight. [7] **And they shall take some of the blood and put it on the two doorposts and on the lintel of the houses where they eat it.** [8] Then they shall eat the flesh on that night; roasted in fire, with unleavened bread and with bitter herbs they shall eat it. [9] Do not eat it raw, nor boiled at all with water, but roasted in fire—its head with its legs and its entrails. [10] You shall let none of it remain until morning, and what remains of it until morning you shall burn with fire. [11] And thus you shall eat it: with a belt on your waist, your sandals on your feet, and your staff in your hand. So you shall eat it in haste. It is the Lord's Passover. [12] For I will pass through the land of Egypt on that night, and will strike all the firstborn in the land of Egypt, both man and beast; and against all the gods of Egypt I will execute judgment: I am the Lord. [13] **Now the blood shall be a sign for you on the houses where you are. And when I see the blood, I will pass over you; and the plague shall not be on you to destroy you** when I strike the land of Egypt. [14] So this day shall be to you a memorial; and you shall keep it as a feast to the Lord throughout your generations. You shall keep it as a feast by an everlasting ordinance.

4. **Second Peter 1:12**— For this reason I will not be negligent to remind you always of these things, though you know and are established in the **present truth.**

5. **Second Peter 1:20-21**— Knowing this first, that **no prophecy of Scripture is of any private interpretation,** ²¹ for **prophecy never came by the will of man,** but **holy men of God spoke as they were moved by the Holy Spirit.**

6. **Psalm 102:18**— This will be **written for the generation to come,** that a people yet to be created may praise the Lord.

7. **Numbers 25:6-13**— And indeed, one of the children of Israel came and **presented to his brethren a Midianite woman in the sight of Moses and in the sight of all the congregation of the children of Israel, who were weeping at the door of the tabernacle of meeting.** ⁷ Now when **Phinehas** the son of Eleazar, the son of Aaron the priest, saw it, he rose from among the congregation and **took a javelin in his hand;** ⁸ **and he went after the man of Israel into the tent and thrust both of them through,** the man of Israel, and the woman through her body. **So the plague was stopped among the children of Israel.** ⁹ And those who died in the plague were twenty-four thousand. ¹⁰ Then the Lord spoke to Moses, saying: ¹¹ "Phinehas the son of Eleazar, the son of Aaron the priest, has turned back My wrath from the children of Israel, because he was zealous with My zeal among them, so that I did not consume the children of Israel in My zeal. ¹² Therefore say, 'Behold, I give to him My covenant of peace; ¹³ and **it shall be to him and his descendants after him a covenant of an everlasting priesthood, because he was zealous for his God,** and made atonement for the children of Israel.'"

8. **First Maccabees 2:16-29 New Revised Standard Version**— Many from Israel came to them; and Mattathias and his sons were assembled. ¹⁷ Then the king's officers spoke to Mattathias as follows: "You are a leader, honored and great in this town, and supported by sons and brothers. ¹⁸ Now be the first to come and do what the king commands, as all the Gentiles and the people of Judah and those that are left in Jerusalem have done. Then you and your sons will be among the friends of the king, and you and your sons will be honored with silver and gold and many gifts." ¹⁹ But Mattathias answered and said in a loud voice: "Even if all the nations that live under the rule of the king obey him, and have chosen to do his commandments, every one of them abandoning the religion of their ancestors, ²⁰ I and my sons and my brothers will live by the covenant of our ancestors. ²¹ Far be it from us to desert the law and the ordinances. ²² We will not obey the king's words by turning aside from our religion to the right hand or to the left." ²³ When he had finished speaking these words, a Jew came forward in the sight of all to offer sacrifice upon the altar in Modein, according to the king's command. ²⁴ When Mattathias **saw it, he be burned with zeal and his heart was stirred.** He gave vent to righteous anger; he ran and killed him upon the altar. ²⁵ At the same time he killed the king's officer who was forcing them to sacrifice, and he tore down the altar. ²⁶ **Thus he burned with zeal for the law, as Phinehas did against Zimri the son of Salu.** ²⁷ Then Mattathias cried out in the town with a loud voice, saying: "Let every one who is zealous for the law and supports the covenant come out with me!" ²⁸ And he and his sons fled to the hills and left all that they had in the town. ²⁹ At that time many who were seeking righteousness and justice went down to the wilderness to live there.

9. **Second Peter 3:8**— But, beloved, do not forget this one thing, that with the Lord one day is as a thousand years, and a thousand years as one day.

10. **Psalm 90:4**— For a thousand years in Your sight are like yesterday when it is past, and like a watch in the night.

11. **Luke 18:8**— I tell you that He will avenge them speedily. Nevertheless, when the Son of Man comes, will He really find faith on the earth?

12. **Matthew 23:37**— O Jerusalem, Jerusalem, the one who kills the prophets and stones those who are sent to her! How often I wanted to gather your children together, as a hen gathers her chicks under her wings, but you were not willing!

13. **Matthew 3:15 NIV**— Jesus replied, "Let it be so now; it is proper for us to do this to fulfill all righteousness." Then John consented.

14. **Matthew 24:20**— And pray that your flight may not be in winter or on the Sabbath.

15. **Second Peter 3:11-12**— Therefore, since all these things will be dissolved, what manner of persons ought you to be in holy conduct and godliness, [12] looking for and **hastening the coming of the day of God,** because of which the heavens will be dissolved, being on fire, and the elements will melt with fervent heat?

SENSUS PLENIOR

There is a phrase first used in the 1920s labeled *Sensus Plenior*. It is a *Latin phrase* that means a *fuller sense* or *a fuller meaning*. It is a way to define something as holding a deeper, fuller meaning. *Sensus plenior*, by its definition, has a significant space within prophecy. It also relates (at least in part) to much of the Jewish mind, which sees prophecy as a *pattern*.

PROPHECY AS PATTERN

Prophecy exists throughout Scripture and has been declared at least once, in its context, for that time and event in which it was spoken and written. It may then apply again for *another time* and a *similar event* in the future—thus, a pattern. Please list a few examples of this by using scripture references and a brief description.

_____

_____

_____

_____

_____

_____

_____

_____

BEYOND THE PREDICTION FULFILLMENT MOTIF

What is the difference between the Western way of thinking versus the Eastern way of thinking when they hear the words "prophecy" or "prophetic"?

_____

_____

_____

_____

_____

_____

_____

EXAMPLE OF PROPHECY AS A PATTERN USING THE PASSOVER

Deeper, Fuller Meaning

When you have a deeper, fuller understanding of Scripture, you will begin to see patterns throughout the Bible. How is the Messianic prophecy of the Lamb of God from the historical Passover fulfilled by Jesus?

_____

_____

_____

_____

_____

_____

Blood of the Lamb

From blood on the doorposts, blood on a cross, and His blood covering us, a pattern is concealed in one distinct truth and symbolic action and is powerfully revealed in the fulfillment of that action.

FOCUS POINT

Applying the blood of Jesus to your heart and life is vital for your eternal future. It's also vital for your life here on earth. When the Israelites applied the blood of the lamb to their doorposts, it brought protection to everyone in their home. Take this time and pray for your family members. Give them to the Lord and ask Him to reveal Himself to them in a way that will change their lives. Write their names below.

_____

_____

_____

_____

_____

_____

_____

PRESENT TRUTH

What is the meaning of "present truth" that Peter refers to in 2 Peter 1:12?

_____

_____

_____

_____

_____

_____

_____

_____

_____

_____

WILLFULLY LIMITED TO SCRIPTURE

Why is it crucial to stay within what the Bible allows?

_____

_____

_____

_____

_____

_____

_____

_____

_____

_____

_____

_____

_____

GENERATIONAL REPETITION: PHINEHAS AND MATTHIAS

In the stories of Phineas and Mattathias, we see a generational repetition of patterns. What is the pattern you see when reading each of their stories?

_____

_____

_____

_____

_____

_____

_____

_____

_____

_____

THE PASSING OF TIME

Time's *gnawing abstractness* can turn a powerful *revealed truth* for one generation into a forgotten formality when a new generation supersedes the former.

Can you think of a situation that this is true, whether in your family or in history? Write about it.

_____

_____

_____

_____

_____

_____

_____

_____

_____

_____

PRESENT TRUTH AND YOUR RESPONSIBILITY

Why are discipleship and servanthood necessary for equipping those around you?

_____

_____

_____

_____

_____

_____

_____

_____

SENSUS PLENIOR THROUGHOUT THE AGES

Why do you think in every generation, the antichrist has had to be prepared to appear? Please list a few people who may have been ready to be the antichrist in their time.

_____

_____

_____

_____

_____

_____

_____

_____

KAIROS MOMENTS, THE FULLNESS OF APPOINTED TIMES

By faith, lay hold of what God has for you and your family today! Agree with His perfect will for your life and watch the things intended to be fulfilled in a previous generation come to pass in your life according to His purpose for you. Yes, your family has a purpose, a destiny. In Jesus' name, I release a revelation of all you are called to seize and walk in now at this time!

PERSONAL REFLECTION

Take this time to write down a prayer for your family and the generations to come. Declare the Word over your family. We have the ability to change the trajectory of time, take this time to stand on the Word and call things that are not as though they are!

_____

_____

_____

_____

_____

_____

_____

_____

_____

_____

_____

_____

_____

_____

_____

_____

_____

_____

_____

_____

_____

_____

_____

_____

_____

_____

_____

_____

_____

_____

_____

CHAPTER ELEVEN

THE MYSTERY OF APPOINTED TIMES AND PEOPLE

SCRIPTURES

1. **Luke 12:54-56**— Then He also said to the multitudes, "Whenever you see a cloud rising out of the west, immediately you say, 'A shower is coming'; and so it is. [55] And when you see the south wind blow, you say, 'There will be hot weather'; and there is. [56] **Hypocrites!** You can discern the face of the sky and of the earth, but **how is it you do not discern this time?**

2. **First Chronicles 12:32**— Of the sons of Issachar who had understanding of the times, to know what Israel ought to do.

3. **Luke 4:5**— Then the devil, taking Him up on a high mountain, showed Him all the kingdoms of the world in a **moment of time.**

4. **Matthew 16:2-3**— He answered and said to them, "When it is evening you say, 'It will be fair weather, for the sky is red'; [3] and in the morning, 'It will be foul weather today, for the sky is red and threatening.' Hypocrites! You know how to discern the face of the sky, but you cannot discern the signs of **the times.**"

5. **Matthew 12:16-17**— Yet He warned them not to make Him known, [17] **that it might be fulfilled which was spoken by Isaiah the prophet.**

6. **Matthew 21:2-5**— Saying to them, "Go into the village opposite you, and immediately you will find a donkey tied, and a colt with her. Loose them and bring them to Me. [3] And if anyone says anything to you, you shall say, 'The Lord has need of them,' and immediately he will send them." [4] **All this was done that it might be fulfilled which was spoken by the prophet,** saying: [5] **"Tell the daughter of Zion, 'Behold, your King is coming to you, lowly, and sitting on a donkey, a colt, the foal of a donkey.'"**

7. **John 19:36-37**— **For these things were done that the Scripture should be fulfilled, "Not one of His bones shall be broken."** [37] And again another Scripture says, **"They shall look on Him whom they pierced."**

8. **Matthew 8:16-17**— When evening had come, they brought to Him many who were demon-possessed. And He cast out the spirits with a word, and healed all who were sick, [17] **that it might be fulfilled which was spoken by Isaiah the prophet,** saying: **"He Himself took our infirmities and bore our sicknesses."**

9. **Luke 24:42-44**— So they gave Him a piece of a broiled fish and some honeycomb. [43] And He took it and ate in their presence. [44] Then He said to them, "These are the words which I spoke to you while I was still with you, that **all things must be fulfilled which were written in the Law of Moses and the Prophets and the Psalms concerning Me."**

10. **Esther 9:27**— The Jews established and imposed it upon themselves and their descendants and all who would join them, that without fail they should celebrate these two days every year, according to the written instructions and **according to the prescribed time.**

11. **Ecclesiastes 3:1**— To everything there is a season, a time for every purpose under heaven:

12. **Ecclesiastes 3:17**— I said in my heart, "God shall judge the righteous and the wicked, for there is a time there for every purpose and for every work."

13. **Ecclesiastes 8:5-6**— He who keeps his command will experience nothing harmful; and a wise man's heart discerns both time and judgment, [6] because for every matter there is a time and judgment, though the misery of man increases greatly.

14. **Proverbs 15:23**— A man has joy by the answer of his mouth, and a word spoken in due season, how good it is!

15. **Matthew 24:1-2**— Then Jesus went out and departed from the temple, and His disciples came up to show Him the buildings of the temple. [2] And Jesus said to them, "Do you not see all these things? Assuredly, I say to you, **not one stone shall be left here upon another, that shall not be thrown down."**

16. **Matthew 24:15-20**— "Therefore when you see the '**abomination of desolation,**' spoken of by Daniel the prophet, standing in the holy place" (whoever reads, let him understand), [16] "then let those who are in Judea flee to the mountains. [17] Let him who is on the housetop not go down to take anything out of his house. [18] And let him who is in the field not go back to get his clothes. [19] But woe to those who are pregnant and to those who are nursing babies in those days! [20] And pray that your flight may not be in winter or on the Sabbath."

17. **Luke 21:20-24**— **But when you see Jerusalem surrounded by armies, then know that its desolation is near.** [21] Then let those who are in Judea flee to the mountains, let those who are in the midst of her depart, and let not those who are in the country enter her. [22] For these are the days of vengeance, that all things which are written may be fulfilled. [23] But woe to those who are pregnant and to those who are nursing babies in those days! For there will be great distress in the land and wrath upon this people. [24] And **they will fall by the edge of the sword, and be led away captive into all nations. And Jerusalem will be trampled by Gentiles until the times of the Gentiles are fulfilled.**

18. **Ecclesiastes 1:9-11**— That which has been is what will be, that which is done is what will be done, and **there is nothing new under the sun.** [10] Is there anything of which it may be said, "See, this is new"? It has already been in ancient times before us. [11] **There is no remembrance of former things, nor will there be any remembrance of things that are to come by those who will come after.**

19. **Matthew 23:37**— O Jerusalem, Jerusalem, the one who kills the prophets and stones those who are sent to her! **How often I wanted** to gather your children together, as a hen gathers her chicks under her wings, **but you were not willing!**

20. **Luke 13:34**— O Jerusalem, Jerusalem, the one who kills the prophets and stones those who are sent to her! How often I wanted to gather your children together, as a hen gathers her brood under her wings, but you were not willing!

21. **Luke 18:8**— I tell you that He will avenge them speedily. Nevertheless, when the Son of Man comes, will He really find faith on the earth?

22. **Second Timothy 4:8 NIV**— Now there is in store for me the crown of righteousness, which the Lord, the righteous Judge, will award to me on that day—and not only to me, but also to **all who have longed for his appearing.**

23. **First Corinthians 15:45**— And so it is written, "**The first man Adam became a living being.**" The last Adam became a life-giving spirit.

24. **Revelation 20:6**— Blessed and holy is he who has part in the first resurrection. Over such the second death has no power, but they shall be priests of God and of Christ, and **shall reign with Him a thousand years.**

25. **Revelation 20:3**— And he cast him into the bottomless pit, and shut him up, and set a seal on him, so that he should deceive the nations no more till the thousand years were finished. But after these things he must be released for a little while.

26. **Revelation 20:5**— But the rest of the dead did not live again until the thousand years were finished. This is the first resurrection.

27. **Revelation 20:7-11**— Now when the thousand years have expired, Satan will be released from his prison. [8] and will go out to deceive the nations which are in the four corners of the earth, Gog and Magog, to gather them together to battle, whose number is as the sand of the sea. [9] They went up on the breadth of the earth and surrounded the camp of the saints and the beloved city. And **fire came down from God out of heaven and devoured them.** [10] **The devil, who deceived them, was cast into the lake of fire and brimstone where the beast and the false prophet are. And they will be tormented day and night forever and ever.** [11] Then I saw a great white throne and Him who sat on it, **from whose face the earth and the heaven fled away.** And there was found no place for them.

28. **Luke 12:54-56**— Then He also said to the multitudes, "Whenever you see a cloud rising out of the west, immediately you say, 'A shower is coming'; and so it is. [55] And when you see the south wind blow, you say, 'There will be hot weather'; and there is. [56] Hypocrites! You can discern the face of the sky and of the earth, but **how is it you do not discern this time?**"

UNDERSTANDING TIME: CHRONOS, KAIROS, EPOCHS

Chronos

1. *Chronos*: A Greek word meaning *a sequential chronological time* or *a particular time and season.*

Kairos

3. *Kairos*: A Greek word meaning *the right, critical, or opportune moment in time.*

How do *kairos* moments connect with the prophetic?

_____

_____

_____

_____

_____

_____

_____

_____

_____

_____

_____

_____

_____

_____

_____

_____

Epoch

3. *Epoch*: is a distinct period in history or a person's life marked by notable events or particular characteristics.

FOCUS POINT

Take this time to think if there has been an *epoch* or a significant event that has taken place in your life. Write it and explain why it is significant to you.

_____
_____
_____
_____
_____
_____
_____
_____
_____
_____
_____
_____
_____
_____
_____

APPOINTED PROPHETIC MOMENTS IN TIME

Joseph lists a few scripture references to Jerusalem's fateful day in AD 70. How can these scriptures be *sensus plenior* and show last days and end-time implications?

_____
_____
_____
_____
_____
_____
_____

HIS-STORY REPEATS ITSELF

What are your thoughts with what Joseph said, "Ecclesiastes states there is *nothing new under the sun*, and it could be that history will repeat itself until the fullness of time has come, or there has been the proper fulfillment of prophecy." Add your thoughts.

_____

_____

_____

_____

_____

_____

_____

_____

THE GREAT PROPHETIC CO-MISSION

What are ways that we can have commission with God in achieving the *Great Commission?*

_____

_____

_____

_____

_____

_____

SOBERING STATEMENTS FOR A KAIROS MOMENT YET TO COME!

Consider the time and season we are living in. How can you eagerly long for Jesus' appearance?

_____

_____

_____

_____

_____

_____

_____

JESUS SHIFTED THE AXIS OF POWER

A Thousand Years to Finish Adam's Assignment

How are Adam, Jesus, and the Millennial Reign connected?

_____

_____

_____

_____

_____

_____

_____

INTERPRETING THE TIMES YOU LIVE IN

According to 1 Chronicles 12:32, what are the three things the sons of Issachar did? Why are those things important for us to do today?

_____
_____
_____
_____
_____
_____
_____
_____
_____

PERSONAL REFLECTION

God doesn't call you to live wherever you choose; you must make sure you are where God has called you. If you don't know for sure, it is vital to seek Him over His will for your life. Take this time to ask the Lord if you are in His will, or if there are new things coming your way that you need to prepare for. Write down what you feel He is saying to you.

_____
_____
_____
_____
_____
_____
_____
_____
_____
_____
_____

SECTION THREE

DARK POWERS AND STRANGE ENCOUNTERS

CHAPTER TWELVE

GATEKEEPERS TO THE SPIRIT REALM

SCRIPTURES

1. **Ezekiel 22:30**— So I sought for a man among them who would make a wall, and **stand in the gap before Me on behalf of the land**, that I should not destroy it; but I found no one.

2. **Genesis 1:3**— Then God said, "Let there be light"; and there was light.

3. **First Timothy 2:14 NIV**— And Adam was not the one deceived; it was the woman who was deceived and became a sinner.

4. **Genesis 3:17**— Then to Adam He said, "Because you have heeded the voice of your wife, and have eaten from the tree of which I commanded you, saying, 'You shall not eat of it': "Cursed is the ground for your sake; in toil you shall eat of it all the days of your life."

5. **First Thessalonians 5:23**— Now may the God of peace Himself sanctify you completely; and may your whole **spirit**, **soul**, and **body** be preserved blameless at the coming of our Lord Jesus Christ.

6. **First Corinthians 15:46**— However, the spiritual is not first, but the natural, and afterward the spiritual.

7. **Romans 10:9**— That if you confess with your mouth the Lord Jesus and believe in your heart that God has raised Him from the dead, you will be saved.

8. **Mark 16:18**— They will lay hands on the sick, and they will recover.

9. **Hebrews 7:8**— Here mortal men receive tithes, but there he receives them, of whom it is witnessed that he lives.

10. **John 3:5**— Jesus answered, "Most assuredly, I say to you, unless one is **born of water** and the Spirit, he cannot enter the kingdom of God."

11. **John 14:9**— Jesus said to him, "Have I been with you so long, and yet you have not known Me, Philip? **He who has seen Me has seen the Father**; so how can you say, 'Show us the Father'?"

12. **Proverbs 20:27**— The spirit of a man is the lamp of the Lord, searching all the inner depths of his heart.

13. **First Corinthians 2:14-15**— But the natural man does not receive the things of the Spirit of God, for they are foolishness to him; nor can he know them, **because they are spiritually discerned.** [15] But he who is spiritual judges all things, yet he himself is rightly judged by no one.

14. **Hebrews 1:3**— Upholding all things by the word of His power.

15. **John 20:22**— And when He had said this, **He breathed on them, and said to them, "Receive the Holy Spirit."**

16. **Hebrews 12:23**— To the general assembly and church of the firstborn who are registered in heaven, to God the Judge of all, **to the spirits of just men made perfect.**

17. **Acts 10:9-13**— The next day, as they went on their journey and drew near the city, Peter went up on the housetop to pray, about the sixth hour. [10] Then he became very hungry and wanted to eat; but while they made ready, he fell into a trance [11] and saw heaven opened and an object like a great sheet bound at the four corners, descending to him and let down to the earth. [12] In it were all kinds of four-footed animals of the earth, wild beasts, creeping things, and birds of the air. [13] And a voice came to him, "Rise, Peter; kill and eat."

18. **Acts 8:39-40**— Now when they came up out of the water, **the Spirit of the Lord caught Philip away,** so that the eunuch saw him no more; and he went on his way rejoicing. [40] But **Philip was found at Azotus.** And passing through, **he preached in all the cities till he came to Caesarea.**

MAN ONCE HAD SIMULTANEOUS ACCESS TO BOTH REALMS

What happened to man after the fall of Adam?

_____

_____

_____

_____

_____

_____

_____

_____

_____

ADAM WILLINGLY
CHOSE REBELLION AGAINST GOD

How do we know that Adam's sin was a *choice* that he made?

_____

_____

_____

_____

_____

_____

_____

Why is it important for us to list our makeup in the order of spirit, soul, and body?

_____

_____

_____

_____

_____

_____

_____

GETTING A SUPERNATURAL REACTION

What does it take to induce a supernatural reaction? Give an example from Scripture to illustrate the point.

_____

_____

_____

_____

_____

_____

_____

PERMISSION AND VETO POWER

Why did Jesus have to come in human form to save the world? Why couldn't He have just destroyed the works of the enemy from His position with the Father?

_____

_____

_____

_____

_____

_____

PHYSICAL BODIES ARE POSITIONS OF AUTHORITY

When a born-again believer fully submits to Jesus, walks as a disciplined follower of the Word of God, and uses their authority—look out, darkness! Because the Kingdom of God is being granted permission to operate!

FOCUS POINT

One of the enemy's biggest fears is when a believer is fully persuaded in the Word of God and believes what it says. This faith that is found is an unwavering faith and this scares the devil and his minions. Take this time to examine your heart and see if this is you or if you need to take steps to become fully persuaded. Write down what is on your heart during this time with the Lord.

_____

_____

_____

_____

_____

_____

_____

CREATION OR CHILDREN

What is the difference between God's creation and God's children?

_____

_____

_____

_____

_____

_____

_____

_____

DEATH DOESN'T COMPUTE WITH ANYONE

We were not created to die. We were created for eternity. Your Great Creator programmed you for eternal thinking. Saying all of that to make the point: Although we live in a natural corporeal body, there is more to us than simply that!

PHILIP'S UNIQUE ENCOUNTER

What happens "When free moral agents surrender to the realm of the spirit, God's way?"

_____

_____

_____

_____

_____

_____

_____

_____

_____

_____

PERSONAL REFLECTION

When we are surrendered to the realm of the spirit God's way, great things can happen. Have you had a moment in your life when you felt the Lord leading you to do something that was hard to understand or maybe out of the normal? Such as Peter visiting the Gentiles. The Lord spoke to Peter after giving him a vision and said he was to go to the Gentiles. Peter obeyed and the Gentiles were welcomed into the body of Christ! Write down your moment when you stepped out after hearing the Holy Spirit guide you.

_____

_____

_____

_____

_____

_____

_____

_____

_____

_____

_____

_____

_____

_____

_____

_____

_____

_____

_____

CHAPTER THIRTEEN

MYSTERIES AND STRANGE HAPPENINGS

SCRIPTURES

1. **First Corinthians 4:1-2**— Let a man so consider us, as servants of Christ and **stewards of the mysteries** of God. [2] Moreover it is required in stewards that one be found faithful.

2. **First Corinthians 2:10**— But God has revealed them to us through His Spirit. For **the Spirit searches all things, yes, the deep things of God.**

3. **First Corinthians 4:6**— …that you may learn in us **not to think beyond what is written**, that none of you may be puffed up on behalf of one against the other.

4. **Second Corinthians 12:1-4**— It is doubtless not profitable for me to boast. I will come to **visions and revelations of the Lord:** [2] I know a man in Christ who fourteen years ago—whether in the body I do not know, or whether out of the body I do not know, God knows—such a one was **caught up to the third heaven.** [3] And I know such a man—whether in the body or out of the body I do not know, God knows—[4] how **he was caught up into Paradise and heard inexpressible words, which it is not lawful for a man to utter.**

5. **Proverbs 25:2**— It is **the glory of God to conceal a matter**, but the **glory of kings is to search out a matter.**

6. **First Corinthians 14:32**— And the spirits of the prophets are subject to the prophets.

7. **First Corinthians 12:10**— To another the working of miracles, to another prophecy, to another **discerning of spirits,** to another different kinds of tongues, to another the interpretation of tongues.

8. **Luke 8:45-46**— And Jesus said, **"Who touched Me?"** When all denied it, Peter and those with him said, "Master, the multitudes throng and press You, and You say, 'Who touched Me?'" [46] But Jesus said, "Somebody touched Me, for I **perceived power going out from Me."**

9. **Second Corinthians 12:12**— Truly the signs of an apostle were accomplished among you with all perseverance, in **signs** and **wonders** and mighty deeds.

10. **John 12:29**— Therefore **the people who stood by and heard it** said that **it had thundered.** Others said, "**An angel has spoken** to Him."

11. **Isaiah 45:15**— Truly **You are God, who hide Yourself**, O God of Israel, the Savior!

12. **Job 4:12-21**— Now a word was secretly brought to me, and my ear received a whisper of it. [13] In disquieting thoughts from the visions of the night, when deep sleep falls on men, [14] fear came upon me, and trembling, which made all my bones shake. [15] Then a spirit passed before my face; the hair on my body stood up. [16] It stood still, but I could not discern its appearance. A form was before my eyes; there was silence; then I heard a voice saying: [17] "Can a mortal be more righteous than God? Can a man be more pure than his Maker? [18] If He puts no trust in His servants, if He charges His angels with error, [19] how much more those who dwell in houses of clay, whose foundation is in the dust, who are crushed before a moth? [20] They are broken in pieces from morning till evening; they perish forever, with no one regarding. [21] Does not their own excellence go away? They die, even without wisdom."

13. **Second Peter 1:20**— Knowing this first, that **no prophecy of Scripture is of any private interpretation.**

14. **Amos 3:7**— Surely the Lord God does nothing, unless **He reveals His secret to His servants the prophets.**

"LABEL CAGING" THE SUPERNATURAL

"Label caging" is simply labeling something to control it, dismiss it, or direct it. Why do you think labeling something via a catchphrase or metaphor is one of religion's favorite mechanism? Write your thoughts.

_____

_____

_____

_____

_____

_____

_____

_____

_____

_____

_____

_____

WHAT DOES THE BIBLE SAY?

Identifying and finding what the Word of God conveys about such things is of great value.

Please remember, no matter how unique or fantastic an experience might be, we *must always stand firmly on the written Word of God*—the ultimate standard of safety and truth.

Read 1 Corinthians 4:6, what does this verse mean to you?

_____

_____

_____

_____

_____

ENCOUNTERS ARE HIGHLY SUBJECTIVE

Why do you think it is so vital to "cast away" anything that doesn't line up with Scripture or violates Scripture?

_____

_____

_____

_____

_____

UNIQUE PHENOMENA

What two things can transpire as onlookers observe the realm of encounters, as it relates to those observing and hearing about various phenomena?

_____

_____

_____

_____

_____

WHY VISIONS, DREAMS, SYMBOLS, AND THE LIKE?

Why do we receive prophetic revelations in dreams, visions, and symbols?

_____

_____

_____

_____

_____

_____

THE SCOPE OF ENCOUNTERS

What must we remember as encounters and experiences present themselves?

_____

_____

_____

_____

_____

_____

CRUCIAL

If you are experiencing encounters, what is _your_ responsibility?

_____

_____

_____

_____

_____

_____

_____

_____

GOD'S WRITTEN WORD IS A PLACE OF REST

Why is the written Word of God so important for someone operating in the prophetic?

_____
_____
_____
_____
_____
_____
_____
_____

YOU ARE SOPHISTICATED

What can cause a delusion to set in your mind?

_____
_____
_____
_____
_____
_____
_____

Focus Point

Joseph explains how delusions can set in when we think of things and make them a reality in our mind. This can lead us to believe in things that aren't real and can also lead to deception. As 1 Corinthians 2:16 says, "For 'who has known the mind of the Lord that he may instruct Him?' But we have the mind of Christ." We need to keep our minds stayed on Christ, for we have the mind of Christ. Have you found yourself thinking upon things and being close to delusion or has delusion already set in? Take this time with the Lord and ask Him to help you renew your mind. Write down whatever the Lord speaks to you.

_____

_____

_____

_____

_____

_____

_____

_____

_____

_____

_____

_____

_____

_____

_____

_____

_____

_____

_____

_____

UNIQUE SUPERNATURAL ENCOUNTERS

Why is controlling yourself important for those who are learning about operating in the prophetic?

_____

_____

_____

_____

_____

_____

_____

_____

Symbolism, Signs, and Strange Encounters

Traffic

Describe what *traffic* is. What is the best way is to navigate it?

_____

_____

_____

_____

_____

_____

_____

Déjà vu

How can you tell the difference between *déjà vu* as a normal occurrence and experiencing *déjà vu* as part of the prophetic realm?

_____

_____

_____

_____

_____

_____

_____

Sensory Issues

Joseph listed a few examples where someone touched him and he received information about these people. Have you had a similar experience? If so, write about it.

_____

_____

_____

_____

_____

_____

_____

Signs, Prophetic Symbolism, Numbers, etc.

What is a sign?

_____

_____

_____

_____

_____

_____

_____

Recurring Numbers

What could it mean if someone sees repeated numbers?

_____

_____

_____

_____

_____

_____

_____

_____

Dreams

Most often, the best person to interpret a dream is the dreamer!

What is the importance of starting a dream journal?

_____

_____

_____

_____

_____

_____

_____

_____

Be Honest with Your Own Heart

What can happen if you violate your own heart by not being honest?

_____
_____
_____
_____
_____
_____
_____

Strange Entities

Encounters with strange entities can happen; however, certain situations can contribute to these experiences. As a practice, we should check our natural disposition and see if what is experienced has a natural explanation.

THEATRICS OF DARKNESS

Why do you think that the devil was throwing a tantrum in Job 4:12-21?

_____
_____
_____
_____
_____
_____
_____

DISESTEEMING THE DEVIL

Why is it so important to keep things simple when it comes to understanding signs?

_____

_____

_____

_____

_____

_____

THE "SPECIAL ONES"

There is a principle in the Word of God that no prophecy of Scripture is of private interpretation. That same principle is true of prophetic encounters. Although the Holy Spirit will undoubtedly speak a personal word to you, there is no such thing as secret knowledge that only you know about as far as revelatory things go.

PERSONAL REFLECTION

In considering the experiences related in this chapter, is there one that is especially familiar to you or one that you have experienced? What was the outcome? How has the study of these types of experiences helped you in reviewing your own experience?

_____

_____

_____

_____

_____

_____

_____

_____

_____

_____

CHAPTER FOURTEEN

ANGELS OF LIGHT AND DOCTRINES OF DEMONS

SCRIPTURES

1. **Colossians 2:18**— Let no one cheat you of your reward, taking delight in false humility and worship of angels, intruding into those things which he has not seen, vainly puffed up by his fleshly mind.

2. **Galatians 1:8**— But even if we, or an angel from heaven, preach any other gospel to you than what we have preached to you, let him be accursed.

3. **Second Corinthians 11:13-15**— For such are false apostles, deceitful workers, transforming themselves into apostles of Christ. [14] And no wonder! For Satan himself transforms himself into an angel of light. [15] **Therefore it is no great thing if his ministers also transform themselves into ministers of righteousness**, whose end will be according to their works.

4. **Revelation 19:10**— And I fell at his feet to worship him. But he said to me, "**See that you do not do that!** I am your fellow servant, and of your brethren who have the testimony of Jesus. Worship God! For the testimony of Jesus is the spirit of prophecy."

5. **Matthew 24:24**— For false christs and false prophets will rise and show great signs and wonders to deceive, if possible, even the elect.

6. **Proverbs 29:2**—When the righteous are in authority, the people rejoice; **but when a wicked man rules, the people groan.**

7. **Proverbs 14:34**— Righteousness exalts a nation, but sin is a reproach to any people.

8. **Matthew 18:18**— Assuredly, I say to you, whatever you bind on earth will be bound in heaven, and whatever you loose on earth will be loosed in heaven.

9. **Second Peter 2:17-19**— These are wells without water, clouds carried by a tempest, for whom is reserved the blackness of darkness forever. [18] For when **they speak great swelling words of emptiness, they allure through the lusts of the flesh, through lewdness, the ones who have actually**

escaped from those who live in error. [19] While **they promise them liberty,** they themselves are slaves of corruption; for by whom a person is overcome, by him also he is brought into bondage.

10. **Hebrews 5:14**— But solid food belongs to those who are of full age, that is, those who **by reason of use have their senses exercised to discern both good and evil.**

11. **Second Corinthians 11:13-15**— For **such are false apostles, deceitful workers, transforming themselves into apostles of Christ.** [14] And no wonder! For **Satan himself transforms himself into an angel of light.** [15] **Therefore it is no great thing if his ministers also transform themselves into ministers of righteousness,** whose end will be according to their works.

12. **Second Corinthians 2:11**— Lest Satan should take advantage of us; for we are not ignorant of his devices.

13. **First Samuel 15:22-23**— So Samuel said: "Has the Lord as great delight in burnt offerings and sacrifices, as in obeying the voice of the Lord? Behold, to obey is better than sacrifice, and to heed than the fat of rams. [23] For **rebellion is as the sin of witchcraft,** and stubbornness is as iniquity and idolatry. Because you have rejected the word of the Lord, He also has rejected you from being king."

14. **First Samuel 28:3-21**— Now **Samuel had died,** and all Israel had lamented for him and buried him in Ramah, in his own city. And Saul had put the mediums and the spiritists out of the land. [4] Then the Philistines gathered together, and came and encamped at Shunem. So Saul gathered all Israel together, and they encamped at Gilboa. [5] **When Saul saw the army of the Philistines, he was afraid, and his heart trembled greatly.** [6] **And when Saul inquired of the Lord, the Lord did not answer him, either by dreams or by Urim or by the prophets.** [7] **Then Saul said to his servants, "Find me a woman who is a medium, that I may go to her and inquire of her." And his servants said to him, "In fact, there is a woman who is a medium at En Dor."** [8] So Saul disguised himself and put on other clothes, and he went, and two men with him; and they came to the woman by night. And he said, **"Please conduct a séance for me, and bring up for me the one I shall name to you."** [9] Then the woman said to him, "Look, you know what Saul has done, how he has cut off the mediums and the spiritists from the land. Why then do you lay a snare for my life, to cause me to die?" [10] And Saul swore to her by the Lord, saying, "As the Lord lives, no punishment shall come upon you for this thing." [11] Then the woman said, "Whom shall I bring up for you?" And he said, "Bring up Samuel for me." [12] **When the woman saw Samuel, she cried out with a loud voice. And the woman spoke to Saul, saying, "Why have you deceived me? For you are Saul!"** [13] And the king said to her, "Do not be afraid. What did you see?" And the woman said to Saul, "I saw a spirit ascending out of the earth." [14] So he said to her, "What is his form?" And she said, "An old man is coming up, and he is covered with a mantle." And Saul perceived that it was Samuel, and he stooped with his face to the ground and bowed down. [15] **Now Samuel said to Saul, "Why have you disturbed me by bringing me up?"** And Saul answered, "I am deeply distressed; for the Philistines make war against me, and God has departed from me and does not answer me anymore, neither by prophets nor by dreams. Therefore I have called you, that you may reveal to me what I should do." [16] Then Samuel said: "So why do you ask me, seeing the Lord has departed from you

and has become your enemy? [17] And the Lord has done for Himself as He spoke by me. For the Lord has torn the kingdom out of your hand and given it to your neighbor, David. [18] Because you did not obey the voice of the Lord nor execute His fierce wrath upon Ama- lek, therefore the Lord has done this thing to you this day. [19] Moreover the Lord will also deliver Israel with you into the hand of the Philistines. And tomorrow you and your sons will be with me. The Lord will also deliver the army of Israel into the hand of the Philistines." [20] Immediately Saul fell full length on the ground, and was dreadfully afraid because of the words of Samuel. And there was no strength in him, for he had eaten no food all day or all night. [21] And the woman came to Saul and saw that he was severely troubled, and said to him, "Look, your maidservant has obeyed your voice, and I have put my life in my hands and heeded the words which you spoke to me."

15. **Genesis 11:4-6**— And they said, "Come, let us build ourselves a city, and a tower whose top is in the heavens; let us make a name for ourselves, lest we be scattered abroad over the face of the whole earth." [5] But the Lord came down to see the city and the tower which the sons of men had built. [6] And the Lord said, "Indeed the people are one and they all have one language, and this is what they begin to do; now nothing that they propose to do will be withheld from them."

OUT-OF-BIBLE EXPERIENCES

If someone is surrounded by bad teaching and the influence of sensational mechanisms, improper belief systems can be put into practice. What are the dangers of this?

_____

_____

_____

_____

_____

_____

_____

_____

_____

_____

_____

_____

_____

_____

_____

IF THERE IS A COUNTERFEIT, THERE IS A REAL

Unfortunately, if there is a "real" then there will be a counterfeit. The enemy cannot create, so he replicates. He deceives by giving people a tainted version of the real. When people are so consumed with experiences and seeking them out, irresponsibility can take place. What does the Bible say about those who knowingly lead others astray? Look up some verses and write them.

_____
_____
_____
_____
_____
_____
_____

SELF-DECEPTION

Why is self-deception so tragic; and why is our integrity so critical when experiencing the supernatural?

_____
_____
_____
_____
_____
_____
_____

LEGITIMATE ENCOUNTERS BEAR FRUIT UNTO JESUS

Encounters should bear fruit unto Jesus. We must hold fast to the Word of God when considering the narratives of those who have frequent encounters with the unseen realms and have fantastic tales to substantiate them.

DECEIVING GOD'S PEOPLE

FOCUS POINT

How does the angel of light deceive gullible believers? Have you experienced such a time when you believed a supernatural experience only to find out later that it was false?

_____

_____

_____

_____

_____

_____

_____

_____

_____

_____

_____

_____

_____

_____

_____

_____

_____

_____

_____

_____

Think about the way you felt at that moment and be careful not to let those negative feelings lead you astray. Ask the Lord to help you to have wisdom and discernment to recognize the enemy's schemes.

ANGELS OF LIGHT AND DOCTRINES OF DEMONS

FALSE EXPERIENCES WANTING DARK ACCESS

What is the number-one way in which darkness requests permission? Jot down a few ways you can think of right now to combat those requests.

_____

_____

_____

_____

_____

_____

_____

_____

_____

_____

GENERATIONAL GIFTS
TARGETED BY LIGHT AND DARKNESS

Everyone is born with gifts. Depending on what is filling these gifts, whether the Holy Spirit or a demonic force, will decide how these gifts are used, for light or darkness.

YOU'RE NOT TALKING TO GRANDMA!

What is a familiar spirit and why do people mistake them for a loved one who passed away?

_____

_____

_____

_____

_____

_____

_____

_____

_____

_____

DARKNESS NEEDS COOPERATION

How does darkness get access via permission into people's lives?

_____

_____

_____

_____

_____

PERMISSION TO MANIFEST

Could it be that supernatural dark entities have the ability to appear because so many have given permission to them? What are your thoughts?

_____

_____

_____

_____

_____

THE GODLY AND THE WICKED—BOTH ARE GATEWAYS

Just like God's angels, the servants of fires, respond to the Voice of God working through individuals; demonic entities work through those who take on his persuasion. What happens when an individual gives access to these demonic entities?

_____

_____

_____

_____

_____

PERMISSION BY REQUEST

What is the number-one way a request is made by darkness?

_____

_____

_____

_____

_____

_____

CLOUDS WITHOUT WATER, ETC.

How does 2 Peter 2:17-19 give us insight into the heart of deception and the deceivers?

_____

_____

_____

_____

_____

_____

_____

NO QUENCHING OF THIRST

Explain the following:

   Wells with no water:

_____

_____

_____

_____

_____

_____

Clouds carried by a tempest:

_____

_____

_____

_____

_____

_____

Great swelling words:

_____

_____

_____

_____

_____

_____

SUSCEPTIBLE TO HIGHER FORMS OF EVIL

What is a symptom of a hardened heart?

_____

_____

_____

_____

_____

_____

_____

_____

_____

_____

_____

_____

_____

THE GREAT MIMIC

Why do angels of light and false apostles transform or disguise themselves for deception?

_____

_____

_____

_____

_____

_____

_____

_____

DEALING WITH DECEPTION IS SIMPLE

Satan is the great mimic, always wanting to copycat anything that Jesus does. We cannot be "ignorant of his devices." What does this phrase mean?

_____

_____

_____

_____

_____

_____

_____

_____

REBELLION AS WITCHCRAFT

When taking 1 Samuel 15:22-23 into context, we can ascertain a definition for the phrase, "Rebellion is as the sin of witchcraft." First, we need to recognize that rebellion is a violation of authority.

VIOLATION OF AUTHORITY

How is rebellion tied to a violation of God's authority?

_____

_____

_____

_____

_____

_____

_____

_____

_____

_____

_____

WITCHCRAFT IS AN UNAUTHORIZED USE OF SUPERNATURAL POWER

What were Nimrod and his followers looking to access and what did God do to stop this?

_____

_____

_____

_____

_____

_____

_____

_____

_____

_____

_____

UNAUTHORIZED ACCESS TO
THE REALM OF THE SPIRIT

What are the three unauthorized violations of authority that can help you discern the truth about a supernatural experience?

_____

_____

_____

_____

_____

KEEPING PROPHECY CLEAN

What could be the first step into becoming a false witness, false voice, and, God forbid, a false prophet?

_____

_____

_____

_____

_____

_____

THE WORD OF GOD WILL CHECK YOU

How can someone develop a calloused heart?

_____

_____

_____

_____

_____

_____

UNCALLOUSED MATURITY

PERSONAL REFLECTION

When operating in the prophetic, we must maintain our integrity and be honest with ourselves and those around us. How can you use the Word of God to check yourself in keeping prophecy clean? Take this time to examine your heart; if you have ever violated self-honesty, repent, and ask God to help you learn faith with honesty.

SECTION FOUR

RIGHTSIZING THE PROPHETIC

CHAPTER FIFTEEN

HARNESSING THE EXPERIENCE

SCRIPTURES

1. **Hebrews 5:14**— But solid food belongs to those who are of full age, that is, those who by reason of use **have their senses exercised** to discern both good and evil.

2. **First Corinthians 4:6 NIV**— …so that you may learn from us the meaning of the saying, "Do not go beyond what is written." Then you will not be puffed up in being a follower of one of us over against the other.

3. **Ecclesiastes 7:20-22**— For there is not a just man on earth who does good and does not sin. ^{21} Also do not take to heart everything people say, lest you hear your servant cursing you. ^{22} For many times, also, your own heart has known that even you have cursed others.

4. **Amos 3:7**— Surely the Lord God does nothing, unless He **reveals His secret** to His servants the prophets.

5. **Isaiah 66:1-2**— Thus says the Lord: "Heaven is My throne, and earth is My footstool. Where is the house that you will build Me? And where is the place of My rest? ^{2} For all those things My hand has made, and all those things exist," says the Lord. "**But on this one will I look: on him who is poor and of a contrite spirit, and who trembles at My word.**"

6. **James 4:6**— But He gives more grace. Therefore He says: "God resists the proud, but gives grace to the humble."

7. **Second Timothy 3:16-17**— All Scripture is given by inspiration of God, and is profitable for doctrine, for reproof, for correction, for instruction in righteousness, ^{17} that the man of God may be complete, thoroughly equipped for every good work.

8. **First Corinthians 14:32**— And the **spirits of the prophets are subject to the prophets.**

9. **First Corinthians 14:32 NIV**— The spirits of prophets are subject to the control of prophets.

10. **Matthew 9:3-4**— And at once some of the scribes said within themselves, "This Man blasphemes!" ^{4} But **Jesus, knowing their thoughts**, said, "Why do you think evil in your hearts?

11. **Luke 6:8**— But **He knew their thoughts,** and said to the man who had the withered hand, "Arise and stand here." And he arose and stood.

12. **First Corinthians 2:10-11 NIV**— These are the things God has revealed to us by his Spirit. The Spirit searches all things, even the deep things of God. [11] For who knows a person's thoughts except their own spirit within them? In the same way no one knows the thoughts of God except the Spirit of God.

13. **Genesis 18:10-15 NIV**— Then one of them said, "I will surely return to you about this time next year, and Sarah your wife will have a son." Now Sarah was listening at the entrance to the tent, which was behind him. [11] Abraham and Sarah were already very old, and Sarah was past the age of childbearing. [12] So Sarah laughed to herself as she thought, "After I am worn out and my lord is old, will I now have this pleasure?" [13] Then the Lord said to Abraham, "Why did Sarah laugh and say, 'Will I really have a child, now that I am old?' [14] Is anything too hard for the Lord? I will return to you at the appointed time next year, and Sarah will have a son." [15] Sarah was afraid, so she lied and said, "I did not laugh." But he said, "Yes, you did laugh."

14. **Acts 8:18-24 NIV**— When Simon saw that the Spirit was given at the laying on of the apostles' hands, he offered them money [19] and said, "Give me also this ability so that everyone on whom I lay my hands may receive the Holy Spirit." [20] Peter answered: "May your money perish with you, because you thought you could buy the gift of God with money! [21] You have no part or share in this ministry, because your heart is not right before God. [22] Repent of this wickedness and pray to the Lord in the hope that he may forgive you for having such a thought in your heart. [23] **For I see that you are full of bitterness and captive to sin.**" [24] Then Simon answered, "Pray to the Lord for me so that nothing you have said may happen to me."

15. **First Corinthians 14:22-25**— Therefore tongues are for a sign, not to those who believe but to unbelievers; but prophesying is not for unbelievers but for those who believe. [23] Therefore if the whole church comes together in one place, and all speak with tongues, and there come in those who are uninformed or unbelievers, will they not say that you are out of your mind? [24] But if all prophesy, and an unbeliever or an uninformed person comes in, he is convinced by all, he is convicted by all. [25] And thus the secrets of his heart are revealed; and so, falling down on his face, he will worship God and report that God is truly among you.

16. **First Corinthians 5:1-13**— It is actually reported that there is sexual immorality among you, and such sexual immorality as is not even named among the Gentiles—that a man has his father's wife! [2] And you are puffed up, and have not rather mourned, that he who has done this deed might be taken away from among you. [3] For I indeed, as absent in body but present in spirit, have already judged (as though I were present) him who has so done this deed. [4] In the name of our Lord Jesus Christ, when you are gathered together, along with my spirit, with the power of our Lord Jesus Christ, [5] deliver such a one to Satan for the destruction of the flesh, that his spirit may be saved in the day of the Lord Jesus. [6] Your glorying is not good. Do you not know that a little leaven leavens the whole lump? [7] Therefore purge out the old leaven, that you may be a new lump, since you truly are unleavened. For indeed Christ, our Passover, was sacrificed for us. [8] Therefore let us keep the

feast, not with old leaven, nor with the leaven of malice and wickedness, but with the unleavened bread of sincerity and truth. [9] I wrote to you in my epistle not to keep company with sexually immoral people. [10] Yet I certainly did not mean with the sexually immoral people of this world, or with the covetous, or extortioners, or idolaters, since then you would need to go out of the world. [11] But now I have written to you not to keep company with anyone named a brother, who is sexually immoral, or covetous, or an idolater, or a reviler, or a drunkard, or an extortioner—not even to eat with such a person. [12] For what have I to do with judging those also who are outside? Do you not judge those who are inside? [13] But those who are outside God judges. Therefore "put away from yourselves the evil person."

17. **First Corinthians 6:12-20**— All things are lawful for me, but all things are not helpful. All things are lawful for me, but I will not be brought under the power of any. [13] Foods for the stomach and the stomach for foods, but God will destroy both it and them. Now the body is not for sexual immorality but for the Lord, and the Lord for the body. [14] And God both raised up the Lord and will also raise us up by His power. [15] Do you not know that your bodies are members of Christ? Shall I then take the members of Christ and make them members of a harlot? Certainly not! [16] Or do you not know that he who is joined to a harlot is one body with her? For "the two," He says, "shall become one flesh." [17] But he who is joined to the Lord is one spirit with Him. [18] Flee sexual immorality. Every sin that a man does is outside the body, but he who commits sexual immorality sins against his own body. [19] Or do you not know that your body is the temple of the Holy Spirit who is in you, whom you have from God, and you are not your own? [20] For you were bought at a price; therefore glorify God in your body and in your spirit, which are God's.

18. **Psalm 119:11**— Your word I have hidden in my heart, that I might not sin against You.

19. **Romans 10:17**— So then faith comes by hearing, and hearing by the word of God.

What is the importance of having your character empowered by the Word of God?

_____

_____

_____

_____

_____

_____

_____

_____

_____

_____

SUPERSTITION

What is the main reason that people will believe a superstition? Have you ever been in a place where you did or almost fell into the snares of superstition? Based on 1 Corinthians 4:6, what does this verse stress that we should not do, and how do we apply this to superstition?

_____
_____
_____
_____
_____
_____
_____
_____
_____
_____

TRAINING IS IN ORDER

Why is it so important that prophetic gifts have training and practice? If there is no training, what is the result?

_____
_____
_____
_____
_____
_____
_____
_____
_____
_____
_____

EMOTIONAL INTELLIGENCE

How can you tell if someone has *emotional intelligence?*

_____

_____

_____

_____

_____

_____

_____

_____

UNBEARABLE EMOTIONS

FOCUS POINT

At times in our lives, we can be faced with intense *traffic* (experiencing supernatural data and amplified emotions). Have you ever experienced this to the degree that it caused hurt and you wanted to withdraw? If so, explain the situation. Ask the Lord to speak to you and minister healing to your heart. If you have any unforgiveness toward the situation, take this time to forgive those who have caused you pain.

_____

_____

_____

_____

_____

_____

_____

_____

_____

_____

TRAIN PAST THE PAIN

What are the tools we can use to *train past the pain* and can be a tremendous source of life regarding intense traffic?

_____

_____

_____

_____

_____

_____

_____

_____

_____

_____

_____

_____

_____

CAN HE TRUST YOU WITH HIS SECRETS?

What type of person does the Lord trust with His secrets?

_____

_____

_____

_____

_____

_____

_____

_____

_____

_____

_____

_____

THE POWER OF HUMILITY

What causes God's attention to come upon you and is a safety feature to keep the prophetic person's mind stable?

_____

_____

_____

_____

_____

_____

_____

_____

MUST DIE TO SELF

When you hear the phrase, "must die to self," what does this look like to you?

_____

_____

_____

_____

_____

_____

_____

STOP BEING SO SENSITIVE

Having a heart not grounded in the Word of God can lead people to be overly sensitive. Allow the Word to help rightsize your heart and bring correction. As 2 Timothy 3:17 says, "That the man of God may be complete, thoroughly equipped for every good work."

PROPHETIC PEOPLE CAN CONTROL THEIR GIFT

Some have asked, "Why me, why do I see or experience these things?" One of the reasons is because your gift is working whether you are trying or not. The ability is God-given and has always been with you. This is why we need to master the experience and learn to control the gifts inside you.

RELAYING A REVELATION

List a few reasons why prophecies sometimes fail.

_____

_____

_____

_____

_____

_____

_____

_____

IF ALL PROPHESY

How does 1 Corinthians 14, describe prophecy and who does it say can prophesy?

_____

_____

_____

_____

_____

_____

_____

_____

MANY THINK PROPHECY
IS WEIRD UNTIL

The Lord wants the unbeliever and uniformed person to experience Him. How does He do this according to 1 Corinthians 14:25?

_____

_____

_____

_____

_____

_____

OFFICE AND GIFT ARE NOT THE SAME

What is the ultimate responsibility of any office gift listed in Ephesians 4:11?

_____

_____

_____

_____

_____

_____

GAIN SAYING

How can self-deception take root if gain saying becomes practice in someone's life?

_____

_____

_____

_____

_____

_____

THE BEST FORM
OF DELIVERANCE

It is so important for the believer to have healthy teaching. Sound biblical teaching from a pastor-teacher is necessary to walk in the highest form of deliverance. If you have a local church, or you follow someone online, what are ways that you receive your teachings for growth and deliverance?

_____

_____

_____

_____

_____

_____

_____

_____

_____

_____

_____

TORTURING THE DATA WILL GET A
CONFESSION YOU DON'T WANT

What can create a culture of dysfunction?

_____

_____

_____

_____

_____

_____

_____

_____

_____

_____

_____

IMMORALITY AND GIFTS

According to 1 Corinthians 5:1-13, Paul was bringing correction to the church of Corinth. Write down your thoughts concerning verse 6, "Do you not know that a little leaven leavens the whole lump?"

_____

_____

_____

_____

_____

_____

_____

_____

_____

_____

_____

_____

FLEE SEXUAL IMMORALITY

Why is it a costly mistake to put more emphasis on the supernatural than the Word of God?

_____

_____

_____

_____

_____

_____

_____

_____

_____

_____

_____

HYSTERIA IS COUNTERED BY A LOVE OF THE TRUTH

PERSONAL REFLECTION

Harnessing your emotions and experiences, by having a foundation of unshakable trust in the Word of God, is so important so that immorality and a misguided culture doesn't occur. Take this personal reflection time and write down some verses that have helped you harness your emotions and experiences.

_____
_____
_____
_____
_____
_____
_____
_____
_____
_____
_____
_____
_____
_____
_____
_____
_____
_____
_____
_____
_____
_____

CHAPTER SIXTEEN

THE COUNTERFEIT ANOINTING

SCRIPTURES

1. **First John 2:27**— But the anointing which you have received from Him abides in you, and you do not need that anyone teach you; but as the same anointing teaches you concerning all things, and is true, and is not a lie, and just as it has taught you, you will abide in Him.

2. **First John 2:27 NIV**— As for you, the anointing you received from him remains in you, and you do not need anyone to teach you. But as his anointing teaches you about all things and as that anointing is **real, not counterfeit**—just as it has taught you, remain in him.

3. **James 3:15**— This wisdom does not descend from above, but is earthly, sensual, demonic.

4. **Hebrews 12:16**— Lest there be any fornicator or profane person like Esau, who for one morsel of food sold his birthright.

5. **Hebrews 12:16 NASB1977**— That there be no immoral or godless person like Esau, who sold his own birthright for a single meal.

6. **First Kings 13:17-19, 23-24 NASB1995**— For **a command came to me by the word of the Lord, "You shall eat no bread, nor drink water there; do not return by going the way which you came."** [18] He said to him, "I also am a prophet like you, and **an angel spoke to me** by the word of the Lord, saying, **'Bring him back with you to your house, that he may eat bread and drink water.'**" But **he lied to him.** [19] So he went back with him, and ate bread in his house and drank water. [23] It came about after he had eaten bread and after he had drunk, that he saddled the donkey for him, for the prophet whom he had brought back. [24] Now when he had gone, a lion met him on the way and killed him, and his body was thrown on the road, with the donkey standing beside it; the lion also was standing beside the body.

7. **Leviticus 6:12-13**— And the fire on the altar shall be kept burning on it; it shall not be put out. And the priest shall burn wood on it every morning and lay the burnt offering in order on it; and he

shall burn on it the fat of the peace offerings. [13] A fire shall always be burning on the altar; it shall never go out.

8. **Leviticus 9:23-24**— And Moses and Aaron went into the tabernacle of meeting and came out and blessed the people. Then the glory of the Lord appeared to all the people, [24] and fire came out from before the Lord and consumed the burnt offering and the fat on the altar. When all the people saw it, they shouted and fell on their faces.

9. **Leviticus 10:1**— Then Nadab and Abihu, the sons of Aaron, each took his censer and put fire in it, put incense on it, and offered profane fire before the Lord, which He had not commanded them.

10. **Acts 8:18-22**— And **when Simon saw that through the laying on of the apostles' hands the Holy Spirit was given, he offered them money,** [19] saying, **"Give me this power also, that anyone on whom I lay hands may receive the Holy Spirit."** [20] But Peter said to him, "Your money perish with you, because **you thought that the gift of God could be purchased with money!** [21] You have neither part nor portion in this for your heart is not right in the sight of God. [22] Repent therefore of this your wickedness, and pray God if perhaps the thought of your heart may be forgiven you."

11. **Proverbs 12:1**— Whoever loves instruction loves knowledge, but he who hates correction is stupid.

12. **Isaiah 8:12 NASB1995**— You are not to say, "It is a conspiracy!" In regard to all that this people call a conspiracy, and you are not to fear what they fear or be in dread of it.

13. **Matthew 6:22-23 NASB1977**— The lamp of the body is the eye; if therefore your eye is clear, your whole body will be full of light. [23] But if your eye is bad, your whole body will be full of darkness. If therefore the light that is in you is darkness, how great is the darkness!

14. **James 1:23**— For if anyone is a hearer of the word and not a doer, he is like a man observing his natural face in a mirror.

15. **Psalm 27:4**— One thing I have desired of the Lord, that will I seek: That I may dwell in the house of the Lord all the days of my life, to **behold** the beauty of the Lord, and to inquire in His temple.

16. **Hebrews 5:14**— But solid food belongs to those who are of full age, that is, those who by reason of use have their senses exercised to discern both good and evil.

17. **Romans 12:2 NASB1977**— And do not be conformed to this world, but be transformed by the renewing of your mind, that you may prove what the will of God is, that which is good and acceptable and perfect.

18. **Matthew 5:8**— Blessed are the pure in heart, for they shall see God.

CHRISTIAN MYSTICISM

We know that when there is a real anointing, there is also a false or counterfeit anointing. Why is this? Because the enemy is a hijacker of anything authentic. He cannot create, so what does he do? He copies and perverts the original. Why are Christian mystics susceptible to falling for a false narrative versus identifying the real?

_____

_____

_____

_____

_____

_____

_____

_____

_____

_____

JACOB MIMICKED
HIS OLDER BROTHER

Hebrews 12:16 (NASB1995) calls Esau "godless" because he reduced his birthright to mean nothing more than a bowl of stew. He sold his birthright to Jacob for food! This was a serious travesty! False anointings are birthed in a culture of dishonor. How do we honor God by honoring the gifts He has given us?

_____

_____

_____

_____

_____

_____

_____

_____

_____

A TALE OF TWO PROPHETS

FOCUS POINT

It is so important to know the Voice of God for yourself. It's also very vital to obey His Voice as He leads you through this life. There will be many false anointings that will try to be His Voice to you, such as the older prophet in 1 Kings 13:17-19. Without obedience to God's Voice, one might easily be led astray by another voice. Take this Focus Point to spend time with the Lord and learn His Voice even more. He will speak if you listen. Read Jeremiah 29:13.

_____

_____

_____

_____

_____

_____

_____

_____

_____

_____

_____

_____

_____

_____

_____

_____

_____

_____

_____

_____

_____

_____

STRANGE FIRE

One of the cloaks of a false anointing is strange fire. In the Old Testament, we see that a fire not ignited by God was referred to as strange fire. This fire was man-made, which went against everything that the Lord commanded. Give examples from today's world of what a "strange fire" might look like.

_____

_____

_____

_____

_____

_____

_____

_____

_____

_____

COUNTERFEITS RISE ON
THE COATTAILS OF THE REAL

The anointing can be very "attractive" to some observers. So much so, they will try to recreate or reproduce that same anointing. It's a matter of the heart and those who carry the real anointing have paid the price for that anointing. What do you think are ways that show someone has paid a price for a real anointing?

_____

_____

_____

_____

_____

_____

_____

_____

_____

_____

SIMON THE SORCERER

Describe what Joseph means by the *snowball effect*.

_____

_____

_____

_____

_____

_____

_____

_____

FALSE ANOINTING AND
SPIRITUAL ENCOUNTERS

Having no discernment can lead to deception. Explain the process and how this deception can come.

_____

_____

_____

_____

_____

_____

_____

_____

_____

_____

_____

_____

_____

_____

RIGHTSIZING A FALSE ANOINTING

Why does darkness fear a believer who is baptized in the washing of His Word?

_____

_____

_____

_____

_____

A FALSE ANOINTING DOES ALL THE RIGHT THINGS FOR THE WRONG REASONS

What is needed to help a naïve person who is walking in a false anointing?

_____

_____

_____

_____

_____

CONSPIRACIES HIJACK WHAT YOUR FAITH IS DESIGNED TO DO

Having access to unlimited data can lead to innumerable amounts of hours spent online. In this time in history, we are exposed to more conspiracies, and it is harder to tell if one is real or fake. The more time you spend searching out conspiracies, the more time you are not in the Word. Why do you think it is so easy to fall prey to the countless hours of conspiracy trails and how can we avoid giving our time away to these things?

_____

_____

_____

_____

_____

THE ANSWER FOR EVERY BELIEVER
IS TO POLISH THE GLASS

What are ways that you can "polish" your soul so that it is not "cluttered"?

_____

_____

_____

_____

_____

_____

THE MIRROR

James 1:23 describes the Word of God as a type of mirror; upon gazing into this mirror, how does transformation come?

_____

_____

_____

_____

_____

_____

BEHOLDING

What are ways to practice "beholding"?

_____

_____

_____

_____

_____

_____

THE FIVE SENSES

According to Hebrews 5:14, how do you polish the glass or mirror?

_____

_____

_____

_____

_____

MIND RENEWAL

What are ways that you are renewing your mind and how has this kept you from being conformed to this world?

_____

_____

_____

_____

_____

_____

MIRROR OR MIRAGE

When someone falls for the mirage, rather than looking into the mirror, what difficulties will inevitably arise?

_____

_____

_____

_____

_____

_____

The Mirror Exposes the Mirage

The gospel that is working through you is the mirror that will expose every mirage! Praise God for the Word!

REAL TRANSFORMATION

PERSONAL REFLECTION

When you soak and meditate on the reflection the mirror presents, you will see the change that has already been done inside you and manifests to the outside! For this Personal Reflection, go to a mirror and look at yourself. Everyone has an opinion about what they see when looking in the mirror. Ask the Lord to speak to you about what He sees; let Him speak His truth to you and then write what He says. The Lord loves you and sees you in ways that you or others might not see. Let His thoughts become yours. (Read Psalm 139:14.)

_____

_____

_____

_____

_____

_____

_____

_____

_____

_____

_____

_____

_____

_____

_____

_____

_____

_____

CHAPTER SEVENTEEN

FALSE PROPHETS

SCRIPTURES

1. **Matthew 24:11 NIV**— And many false prophets will appear and will deceive many people.

2. **Second Peter 2:1-3**— But there were also **false prophets** among the people, even as there will be **false teachers** among you, who will secretly bring in destructive heresies, even denying the Lord who bought them, and bring on themselves swift destruction. ² And many will follow their destructive ways, because of whom the way of truth will be blasphemed. ³ **By covetousness they will exploit you with deceptive words**; for a long time, their judgment has not been idle, and their destruction does not slumber.

3. **Second Thessalonians 2:9-12**— The coming of the lawless one is according to the working of Satan, with all power, signs, and lying wonders, ¹⁰ and with all unrighteous deception among those who perish, because **they did not receive the love of the truth**, that they might be saved. ¹¹ And for this reason God will send them strong delusion, that they should believe the lie, ¹² that they all may be condemned who did not believe the truth but had pleasure in unrighteousness.

4. **John 8:31-32**— Then Jesus said to those Jews who believed Him, "If you abide in My word, you are My disciples indeed. ³² And you shall know the truth, and the truth shall make you free."

5. **First Timothy 4:1-2**— Now the Spirit expressly says that in latter times some will depart from the faith, giving heed to deceiving spirits and doctrines of demons, ² speaking lies in hypocrisy, having their own conscience seared with a hot iron.

6. **Matthew 7:21-23**— "Not everyone who says to Me, 'Lord, Lord,' shall enter the kingdom of heaven, but he who does the will of My Father in heaven. ²² Many will say to Me in that day, 'Lord, Lord, have we not **prophesied** in Your name, cast out demons in Your name, and done many wonders in Your name?' ²³ And then I will declare to them, 'I never knew you; depart from Me, you who practice lawlessness!'"

7. **First John 4:1-3**— Beloved, do not believe every spirit, but test the spirits, whether they are of God; because many false prophets have gone out into the world. ² By this you know the Spirit of God: **Every spirit that confesses that Jesus Christ has come in the flesh is of God**, ³ and every

spirit that does not confess that Jesus Christ has come in the flesh is not of God. And this is the spirit of the Antichrist, which you have heard was coming, and is now already in the world.

8. **Revelation 2:24**— Now to you I say, and to the rest in Thyatira, as many as do not have this doctrine, who have not known the depths of Satan, as they say, I will put on you no other burden.

9. **Matthew 7:20**— Therefore by their fruits you will know them.

10. **First Timothy 3:6**— Not a novice, lest being puffed up with pride he fall into the same condemnation as the devil.

11. **Hebrews 4:13**— And there is no creature hidden from His sight, but all things are naked and open to the eyes of Him to whom we must give account.

12. **Luke 6:26**— Woe to you when all men speak well of you, for so did their fathers to the false prophets.

13. **Second Peter 1:20-21**— Knowing this first, that no prophecy of Scripture is of any private interpretation, [21] for prophecy never came by the will of man, but holy men of God spoke as they were moved by the Holy Spirit.

14. **Second Timothy 3:5-7**— Having a form of godliness but denying its power. And from such people turn away! [6] For of this sort are those who creep into households and make captives of gullible women loaded down with sins, led away by various lusts, [7] always learning and never able to come to the knowledge of the truth.

15. **Ezekiel 13:1-16**— And the word of the Lord came to me, saying, [2] "Son of man, prophesy against the prophets of Israel who prophesy, and say to those who prophesy out of their own heart, 'Hear the word of the Lord!'" [3] Thus says the Lord God: "Woe to the foolish prophets, who follow their own spirit and have seen nothing! [4] O Israel, your prophets are like foxes in the deserts. [5] You have not gone up into the gaps to build a wall for the house of Israel to stand in battle on the day of the Lord. [6] They have envisioned futility and false divination, saying, 'Thus says the Lord!' But the Lord has not sent them; yet they hope that the word may be confirmed. [7] Have you not seen a futile vision, and have you not spoken false divination? You say, 'The Lord says,' but I have not spoken." [8] Therefore thus says the Lord God: "Because you have spoken nonsense and envisioned lies, therefore I am indeed against you," says the Lord God. [9] "My hand will be against the prophets who envision futility and who divine lies; they shall not be in the assembly of My people, nor be written in the record of the house of Israel, nor shall they enter into the land of Israel. Then you shall know that I am the Lord God. [10] Because, indeed, because they have seduced My people, saying, 'Peace!' when there is no peace—and one builds a wall, and they plaster it with untempered mortar— [11] say to those who plaster it with untempered mortar, that it will fall. There will be flooding rain, and you, O great hailstones, shall fall; and a stormy wind shall tear it down. [12] Surely, when the wall has fallen, will it not be said to you, 'Where is the mortar with which you plastered it?'" [13] Therefore thus says the Lord God: "I will cause a stormy wind to break forth in My fury; and there shall be a flooding rain in My anger, and great hailstones in fury to consume it. [14] So I will break down

the wall you have plastered with untempered mortar, and bring it down to the ground, so that its foundation will be uncovered; it will fall, and you shall be consumed in the midst of it. Then you shall know that I am the Lord. [15] Thus will I accomplish My wrath on the wall and on those who have plastered it with untempered mortar; and I will say to you, 'The wall is no more, nor those who plastered it, [16] that is, the prophets of Israel who prophesy concerning Jerusalem, and who see visions of peace for her when there is no peace,'" says the Lord God.

16. **First Timothy 3:1-13**— This is a faithful saying: If a man desires the position of a bishop, he desires a good work. [2] A bishop then must be blameless, the husband of one wife, temperate, sober-minded, of good behavior, hospitable, able to teach; [3] not given to wine, not violent, not greedy for money, but gentle, not quarrelsome, not covetous; [4] one who rules his own house well, having his children in submission with all reverence [5] (for if a man does not know how to rule his own house, how will he take care of the church of God?); [6] not a novice, lest being puffed up with pride he fall into the same condemnation as the devil. [7] Moreover he must have a good testimony among those who are outside, lest he fall into reproach and the snare of the devil. [8] Likewise deacons must be reverent, not double-tongued, not given too much wine, not greedy for money, [9] holding the mystery of the faith with a pure conscience. [10] But let these also first be tested; then let them serve as deacons, being found blameless. [11] Likewise, their wives must be reverent, not slanderers, temperate, faithful in all things. [12] Let deacons be the husbands of one wife, ruling their children and their own houses well. [13] For those who have served well as deacons obtain for themselves a good standing and great boldness in the faith which is in Christ Jesus.

17. **First Samuel 2:12**— Now the sons of Eli were corrupt; they did not know the Lord.

18. **Luke 17:2**— It would be better for him if a millstone were hung around his neck, and he were thrown into the sea, than that he should offend one of these little ones.

19. **Acts 13:6-11**— Now when they had gone through the island to Paphos, they found a certain sorcerer, a false prophet, a Jew whose name was Bar-Jesus, [7] who was with the proconsul, Sergius Paulus, an intelligent man. This man called for Barnabas and Saul and sought to hear the word of God. [8] But Elymas the sorcerer (for so his name is translated) withstood them, seeking to turn the proconsul away from the faith. [9] Then Saul, who also is called Paul, filled with the Holy Spirit, looked intently at him [10] and said, "O full of all deceit and all fraud, you son of the devil, you enemy of all righteousness, will you not cease perverting the straight ways of the Lord? [11] And now, indeed, the hand of the Lord is upon you, and you shall be blind, not seeing the sun for a time." And immediately a dark mist fell on him, and he went around seeking someone to lead him by the hand.

20. **Acts 20:30**— Also, from among yourselves men will rise up, **speaking perverse things**, to draw away the disciples after themselves.

21. **Mark 13:22 KJV**— For false Christs and false prophets shall rise, and shall shew signs and wonders, to **seduce**, if it were possible, even the elect.

22. **Second Corinthians 11:3**— But I fear, lest somehow, as the serpent deceived Eve by his craftiness, so your minds may be corrupted from the simplicity that is in Christ.

23. **Revelation 2:2-3**— I know your works, your labor, your patience, and that you cannot bear those who are evil. And you **have tested those who say they are apostles and are not, and have found them liars**; [3] and you have persevered and have patience, and have labored for My name's sake and have not become weary.

24. **Matthew 6:22**— The lamp of the body is the eye. If therefore your eye is good, your whole body will be full of light.

25. **Jude 1:10-16**— But **these speak evil of whatever they do not know**; and whatever they know naturally, like brute beasts, in these things they corrupt themselves. [11] Woe to them! For they have gone in the **way of Cain**, have run greedily in the **error of Balaam** for profit, and perished in the **rebellion of Korah**. [12] These are spots in your love feasts, while they feast with you without fear, **serving only themselves**. They are clouds without water, carried about by the winds; late autumn trees without fruit, twice dead, pulled up by the roots; [13] raging waves of the sea, foaming up their own shame; wandering stars for whom is reserved the blackness of darkness forever. [14] Now Enoch, the seventh from Adam, prophesied about these men also, saying, "Behold, the Lord comes with ten thousands of His saints, [15] to execute judgment on all, to convict all who are ungodly among them of all their ungodly deeds which they have committed in an ungodly way, and of all the harsh things which ungodly sinners have spoken against Him." [16] These are **grumblers, complainers, walking according to their own lusts; and they mouth great swelling words, flattering people to gain advantage.**

26. **Second Peter 2:1-22**— But there were also **false prophets** among the people, even as there will be **false teachers** among you, who will secretly bring in destructive heresies, even denying the Lord who bought them, and bring on themselves swift destruction. [2] And many will follow their destructive ways, because of whom the way of truth will be blasphemed. [3] By **covetousness they will exploit you with deceptive words**; for a long time their judgment has not been idle, and their destruction does not slumber. [4] For if God did not spare the angels who sinned, but cast them down to hell and delivered them into chains of darkness, to be reserved for judgment; [5] and did not spare the ancient world, but saved Noah, one of eight people, a preacher of righteousness, bringing in the flood on the world of the ungodly; [6] and turning the cities of Sodom and Gomorrah into ashes, condemned them to destruction, making them an example to those who afterward would live ungodly; [7] and delivered righteous Lot, who was oppressed by the filthy conduct of the wicked [8] (for that righteous man, dwelling among them, tormented his righteous soul from day to day by seeing and hearing their lawless deeds)— [9] then the Lord knows how to deliver the godly out of temptations and to reserve the unjust under punishment for the day of judgment, [10] and especially those who **walk according to the flesh** in the **lust of uncleanness** and **despise authority**. They are **presumptuous, self-willed**. They are **not afraid to speak evil of dignitaries,** [11] whereas angels, who are greater in power and might, do not bring a reviling accusation against them before the Lord. [12] But these, like natural brute beasts made to be caught and destroyed, speak evil of the things they do not understand, and will utterly perish in their own corruption, [13] and will receive the wages of unrighteousness, as those who count it pleasure to carouse in the daytime. They are spots and blemishes, carousing in their own deceptions while they feast with you, [14] having eyes

full of adultery and that cannot cease from sin, enticing unstable souls. They have a heart trained in covetous practices, and are accursed children. [15] They have forsaken the right way and gone astray, following the way of Balaam the son of Beor, who loved the wages of unrighteousness; [16] but he was rebuked for his iniquity: a dumb donkey speaking with a man's voice restrained **the madness of the prophet**. [17] These are wells without water, clouds carried by a tempest, for whom is reserved the blackness of darkness forever. [18] For when they speak great swelling words of emptiness, they allure through the lusts of the flesh, through lewdness, the ones who have actually escaped from those who live in error. [19] While they promise them liberty, they themselves are slaves of corruption; for by whom a person is overcome, by him also he is brought into bondage. [20] For if, after they have escaped the pollutions of the world through the knowledge of the Lord and Savior Jesus Christ, they are again entangled in them and overcome, the latter end is worse for them than the beginning. [21] For it would have been better for them not to have known the way of righteousness, than having known it, to turn from the holy commandment delivered to them. [22] But it has happened to them according to the true proverb: "A dog returns to his own vomit," and, "a sow, having washed, to her wallowing in the mire."

27. **Hebrews 5:14**— But solid food belongs to those who re of full age, that is, those who by reason of use have their senses exercised to discern both good and evil.

28. **First Timothy 1:18-20**— This charge I commit to you, son Timothy, according to the prophecies previously made concerning you, that by them you may wage the good warfare, [19] having faith and a good conscience, which some having rejected, concerning the faith have suffered shipwreck, [20] of whom are Hymenaeus and Alexander, whom I delivered to Satan that they may learn not to blaspheme.

29. **Revelation 19:10**— …Worship God! For the testimony of Jesus is the spirit of prophecy.

Why are *lovers of the truth* qualified to venture into the topic of false prophets?

_____

_____

_____

_____

_____

_____

_____

_____

_____

_____

LOVERS OF THE TRUTH

According to John 8:31-32, what makes a legitimate disciple?

_____

_____

_____

_____

_____

_____

CLARITY DEVELOPS AUTHORITY

What happens when you are armed with the truth and in a position of clarity as the Scripture prescribes?

_____

_____

_____

_____

_____

_____

_____

_____

GNOSTICISM

What is Gnosticism? What is the evil deception of this belief?

_____

_____

_____

_____

_____

_____

_____

SOUND DOCTRINE
IS THE ACTUAL TEST

What is the first thing to consider when dealing with false prophets?

_____

_____

_____

_____

_____

_____

PROPHETS ARE EITHER
REAL, NOVICE, OR FALSE

You will know someone is either a real, novice, or false prophet based on their motive. How can you know if someone is a false prophet when examining their fruit?

_____

_____

_____

_____

_____

_____

Real Prophets

What makes a real prophet?

_____

_____

_____

_____

_____

_____

Novice

How do you know if someone is a novice?

_____

_____

_____

_____

_____

False Prophets

What are the dangers of someone entering their hundredfold toward deception?

_____

_____

_____

_____

_____

GOD KNOWS, GOD SEES

FOCUS POINT

In 2 Samuel 23, David desired a drink of water so badly that some of his men went through the enemy's camp and got him a cup of water. David, however, did not drink this cup; rather, he poured it out as a drink offering before the Lord. There are times when the Lord is watching to see if we will pour out what we really desire. Take this time and examine your heart and see if there are things that you have held onto that you should be pouring out before the Lord. Write down anything that comes to you.

_____

_____

_____

_____

_____

_____

_____

_____

_____

_____

_____

_____

_____

_____

_____

_____

_____

_____

_____

_____

_____

_____

_____

MOTIVE

Why do you think a false prophet despises correction?

_____

_____

_____

_____

_____

_____

_____

_____

STRANGE FIRE OF MAN

Having a greater fear of man than fear of God can lead someone to care more about what others think about them than what God says they are to do. We need to be obedient to the Voice of God because this helps develop a true prophet.

FALSE PROPHETS OPERATE IN SELF-WILLED PREDICTIONS

Describe what a self-willed prediction is and why it is dangerous.

_____

_____

_____

_____

_____

_____

_____

_____

_____

_____

FALSE PROPHETS CAUSE LISTENERS TO WANDER

According to Matthew 24:11, many false prophets will cause many to wander. The Oxford Languages definition of *wander* is to walk or move in a leisurely, casual, or aimless way. When someone is led to wander, they have no purpose and no vision, they are aimlessly walking out their lives. False prophets like these types of people. What are ways that we can avoid being a wanderer?

_____

_____

_____

_____

_____

_____

_____

_____

_____

PATTERN-BASED IMMORAL BEHAVIOR

According to Galatians 6, what are ways to restore or help a brother caught in sin?

_____

_____

_____

_____

_____

_____

_____

_____

_____

_____

_____

INSIGHTS INTO FALSE PROPHETS
AND FALSE PROPHECY

False prophets prophesy out of their own hearts. They say what they want, even if they haven't seen anything. In Ezekiel 13:1-16, the Lord addresses these prophets who say there is peace when there is none. He also addresses "one who builds a wall, and they plaster it with untampered mortar." This wall will not stand the wrath that will come, the wind, the hail, and the floods. Why do you think it is so important for prophets to only say what they see?

_____

_____

_____

_____

_____

_____

_____

_____

_____

_____

PATTERNS DETERMINE CAPACITY

Gifting is not what makes a prophet. Write what does make someone a prophet.

_____

_____

_____

_____

_____

_____

_____

_____

_____

QUALIFICATIONS OF A TRUE LEADER

List some qualifications of a true leader as described in 1 Timothy 3:1-13.

_____

_____

_____

_____

_____

_____

_____

_____

LYING TALES AND SUPERNATURAL TRICKERY

False prophets desire a following. They know what they are doing, and they speak perverse things to draw disciples after themselves. Being seductive and using fantastic stories, these false prophets will say and do anything to gather followers. We need to be aware of these schemes and be grounded in the Word so that when these people come into our lives, we will not be led astray by their falsehood.

SPECIAL OR UNCONVENTIONAL
REVELATORY TRAINING

Why do you think Joseph compared the misappropriation of supernatural abilities to a form of witchcraft?

_____

_____

_____

_____

_____

_____

_____

THIRD EYE TRASH

What is "third eye trash," and why should lovers of truth be on guard around false prophets who try to demonstrate the beguiling powers of "opening it"?

_____
_____
_____
_____
_____
_____
_____
_____
_____
_____
_____
_____

DANGER FOR THE NAÏVE

Describe the danger for the naïve person who may be listening to false prophets.

_____
_____
_____
_____
_____
_____
_____
_____
_____
_____
_____

FALSE PROPHETS TALK ABOUT JESUS

What is the goal of the false prophet?

_____

_____

_____

_____

_____

_____

_____

_____

_____

_____

HOW APOSTLES DEAL
WITH FALSE PROPHETS

What can we learn from the stern instructions Paul gave Timothy about false prophets in 1 Timothy 1:18-20? How did Paul describe to Timothy what he did with false prophets?

_____

_____

_____

_____

_____

_____

_____

_____

_____

_____

PERSONAL REFLECTION

False prophets attempt to gather a following of naïve and gullible people. What have you done or plan to do to develop discernment and wisdom concerning identifying a false prophet? Take this time to ask the Lord to speak to you and help you in this time of personal reflection.

_____

_____

_____

_____

_____

_____

_____

_____

_____

_____

_____

_____

_____

_____

_____

_____

_____

_____

_____

_____

_____

_____

_____

_____

_____

_____

_____

SECTION FIVE

AGENTS OF GOD

There was a man sent from God, whose name was John. This man came for a witness, to bear witness of the Light, that all through him might believe.

—**John 1:6-7**

CHAPTER EIGHTEEN

ENCOUNTERING PROPHETS

SCRIPTURES

1. **Hosea 10:12**— Sow for yourselves righteousness; reap in mercy; break up your fallow ground, for it is time to seek the Lord, till He comes and rains righteousness on you.

This chapter is geared to Joseph's personal encounters with the prophetic. The questions in this section will be more personal. Take the time to write down your experiences.

I WANT TO MEET A REAL PROPHET

Have you ever had an encounter with a real prophet? If so, write about your experience.

_____

_____

_____

_____

_____

_____

_____

_____

_____

_____

_____

_____

_____

_____

_____

_____

MY GRANDPARENTS AND MOM KIDNAPPED US AND INTRODUCED US TO A HOLY SPIRIT MEETING!

FOCUS POINT

The story about Joseph's grandparents kidnapping Joseph and his siblings, was the turning point into a series of events that set his life on a collision course with the living God. Take this time to write down a pivotal moment in your life that has shaped who you are today.

_____

_____

_____

_____

_____

_____

_____

_____

_____

_____

_____

_____

_____

_____

_____

_____

_____

_____

_____

_____

_____

PROPHETIC WORD FROM
JOHN PAUL JACKSON

We know that the Lord desires to speak with us on a regular basis and to have that personal one-on-one time with Him. There are, however, times when the Lord will use other people to deliver a special word to us directly from His heart. Have you ever had a word from the Lord given to you by another person? If so, write your word.

_____

_____

_____

_____

_____

_____

_____

_____

_____

PUBLIC WORD OF KNOWLEDGE

Have you been in a situation where you knew you had a word from the Lord for someone? How did you deliver the message, and how was it received?

_____

_____

_____

_____

_____

_____

_____

_____

_____

_____

MY FIRST TRANCE

Joseph shares his very first trance. Have you ever had a trance? Write about it.

_____

_____

_____

_____

_____

_____

_____

_____

_____

_____

VISION ABOUT MARRIAGE

The Lord can confirm in our hearts, through a vision, what His plan is for our lives, as was the case with the vision the Lord gave to Joseph concerning Heather being his wife. Have you ever had a vision that brought confirmation and peace to a decision you needed to make? Write it.

_____

_____

_____

_____

_____

_____

_____

_____

_____

_____

GOD IS ALWAYS SPEAKING

PERSONAL REFLECTION

God is always speaking; the question you must ask yourself is, *Am I always listening?* In Revelation, when Jesus is addressing the seven churches, He says this phrase, "He who has an ear, let him hear what the Spirit says to the churches." There is significance to this phrase. This shows us that many can have ears, yet miss what the Spirit is saying. Take this time to listen and see what the Lord is speaking to you. There are times to speak, and there are times to listen. Write down what you hear Him saying to you.

_____

_____

_____

_____

_____

_____

_____

_____

_____

_____

_____

_____

_____

_____

_____

_____

_____

_____

_____

_____

_____

_____

CHAPTER NINETEEN

OFFICE OF THE PROPHET

SCRIPTURES

1. **Ephesians 4:11** — And He Himself gave some as apostles, some prophets, some evangelists, and some as pastors and teachers.

2. **John 14:24 NIV** — These words you hear are not my own; they belong to the Father who sent me.

3. **Luke 4:16-21 NIV** — He [Jesus] went to Nazareth, where he had been brought up, and on the Sabbath day he went into the synagogue, as was his custom. He stood up to read, [17] and the scroll of the prophet Isaiah was handed to him. Unrolling it, he found the place where it is written: [18] "The Spirit of the Lord is on me, because he has anointed me to proclaim good news to the poor. He has sent me to proclaim freedom for the prisoners and recovery of sight for the blind, to set the oppressed free, [19] to proclaim the year of the Lord's favor." [20] Then he rolled up the scroll, gave it back to the attendant and sat down. The eyes of everyone in the synagogue were fastened on him. [21] He began by saying to them, "Today this scripture is fulfilled in your hearing."

4. **First Samuel 9:9** — (Formerly in Israel, when a man went to inquire of God, he spoke thus: "Come, let us go to the seer"; for he who is now called a prophet was formerly called a seer.)

5. **Deuteronomy 18:20-22** — "But the prophet who presumes to speak a word in My name, which I have not commanded him to speak, or who speaks in the name of other gods, that prophet shall die." [21] And if you say in your heart, "How shall we know the word which the Lord has not spoken?"— [22] when a prophet speaks in the name of the Lord, if the thing does not happen or come to pass, that is the thing which the Lord has not spoken; the prophet has spoken it presumptuously; you shall not be afraid of him.

6. **Ephesians 4:11-12** — And He Himself gave some to be apostles, some prophets, some evangelists, and some pastors and teachers, [12] for the equipping of the saints for the work of ministry, for the edifying of the body of Christ.

7. **First Corinthians 9:2** — If I am not an apostle to others, yet doubtless I am to you. For you are the seal of my apostleship in the Lord.

8. **Acts 27:15-17 KJV** — And when the ship was caught, and could not bear up into the wind, we let her drive. [16] And running under a certain island which is called Clauda, we had much work to

come by the boat: [17] Which when they had taken up, they used helps, undergirding the ship; and, fearing lest they should fall into the quicksands, strake sail, and so were driven.

9. **Acts 11:28**— Then one of them, named Agabus, stood up and showed by the Spirit that there was going to be a great famine throughout all the world, which also happened in the days of Claudius Caesar.

10. **Acts 21:9-11**— Now this man had four virgin daughters who prophesied. [10] And as we stayed many days, a certain prophet named Agabus came down from Judea. [11] When he had come to us, he took Paul's belt, bound his own hands and feet, and said, "Thus says the Holy Spirit, 'So shall the Jews at Jerusalem bind the man who owns this belt, and deliver him into the hands of the Gentiles.'"

11. **Second Samuel 24:11**— Now when David arose in the morning, the word of the Lord came to the prophet Gad, David's seer….

12. **First Chronicles 25:5**— All these were the sons of Heman the king's seer in the words of God, to exalt his horn. For God gave Heman fourteen sons and three daughters.

13. **Second Chronicles 29:25**— And he stationed the Levites in the house of the Lord with cymbals, with stringed instruments, and with harps, according to the commandment of David, of Gad the king's seer, and of Nathan the prophet; for thus was the commandment of the Lord by His prophets.

14. **Second Chronicles 29:29**— And when they had finished offering, the king and all who were present with him bowed and worshiped.

15. **Second Chronicles 9:29**— Now the rest of the acts of Solomon, first and last, are they not written in the book of Nathan the prophet, in the prophecy of Ahijah the Shilonite, and in the visions of Iddo the seer concerning Jeroboam the son of Nebat?

16. **Second Chronicles 12:15**— The acts of Rehoboam, first and last, are they not written in the book of Shemaiah the prophet, and of Iddo the seer concerning genealogies? And there were wars between Rehoboam and Jeroboam all their days.

17. **First Kings 22:22**— The Lord said to him, "In what way?" So he said, "I will go out and be a lying spirit in the mouth of all his prophets." And the Lord said, "You shall persuade him, and also prevail. Go out and do so."

18. **Second Chronicles 18:21-22**— So he said, "I will go out and be a lying spirit in the mouth of all his prophets." And the Lord said, "You shall persuade him and also prevail; go out and do so." [22] Therefore look! The Lord has put a lying spirit in the mouth of these prophets of yours, and the Lord has declared disaster against you.

19. **Ezekiel 13:2,4**— "Son of man, prophesy against the prophets of Israel who prophesy, and say to those who prophesy out of their own heart, 'Hear the word of the Lord!'" [4] O Israel, your prophets are like foxes in the deserts.

20. **Jeremiah 23:13** — And I have seen folly in the prophets of Samaria: They prophesied by Baal and caused My people Israel to err.

21. **Second Chronicles 29:30** — Moreover King Hezekiah and the leaders commanded the Levites to sing praise to the Lord with the words of David and of Asaph the seer. So they sang praises with gladness, and they bowed their heads and worshiped.

22. **Acts 13:1** — Now in the church that was at Antioch there were certain prophets and teachers: Barnabas, Simeon who was called Niger, Lucius of Cyrene, Manaen who had been brought up with Herod the tetrarch, and Saul.

23. **Acts 15:22** — Then it pleased the apostles and elders, with the whole church, to send chosen men of their own company to Antioch with Paul and Barnabas, namely, Judas who was also named Barsabas, and Silas, leading men among the brethren.

24. **Acts 15:27** — We have therefore sent Judas and Silas, who will also report the same things by word of mouth.

25. **Acts 15:32** — Now Judas and Silas, themselves being prophets also, exhorted and strengthened the brethren with many words.

26. **Daniel 9:2** — In the first year of his reign I, Daniel, understood by the books the number of the years specified by the word of the Lord through Jeremiah the prophet, that He would accomplish seventy years in the desolations of Jerusalem.

27. **Jeremiah 25:12** — "Then it will come to pass, when seventy years are completed, that I will punish the king of Babylon and that nation, the land of the Chaldeans, for their iniquity," says the Lord; "and I will make it a perpetual desolation."

28. **Jeremiah 29:10** — For thus says the Lord: After seventy years are completed at Babylon, I will visit you and perform My good word toward you, and cause you to return to this place.

29. **Jeremiah 1:10** — See, I have this day set you over the nations and over the kingdoms, to root out and to pull down, to destroy and to throw down, to build and to plant.

30. **Daniel 5:12** — Inasmuch as an excellent spirit, knowledge, understanding, interpreting dreams, solving riddles, and explaining enigmas were found in this Daniel, whom the king named Belteshazzar, now let Daniel be called, and he will give the interpretation.

31. **Mark 10:37** — Grant us that we may sit, one on Your right hand and the other on Your left, in Your glory.

32. **Luke 9:54** — And when His disciples James and John saw this, they said, "Lord, do You want us to command fire to come down from heaven and consumer them, just as Elijah did?"

33. **Luke 12:48**— But he who did not know, yet committed things deserving of stripes, shall be beaten with few. For everyone to whom much is given, from him much will be required; and to whom much has been committed, of him they will ask the more.

34. **First Kings 20:35-38 NLT**— Meanwhile, the Lord instructed one of the group of prophets to say to another man, "Hit me!" But the man refused to hit the prophet. [36] Then the prophet told him, "Because you have not obeyed the voice of the Lord, a lion will kill you as soon as you leave me." And when he had gone, a lion did attack and kill him. [37] Then the prophet turned to another man and said, "Hit me!" So he struck the prophet and wounded him. [38] The prophet placed a bandage over his eyes to disguise himself and then waited beside the road for the king.

35. **Ephesians 2:20**— Having been built on the foundation of the apostles and prophets, Jesus Christ Himself being the chief cornerstone.

36. **John 5:30-39 NLT**— I can do nothing on my own. I judge as God tells me. Therefore, my judgment is just, because I carry out the will of the one who sent me, not my own will. [31] If I were to testify on my own behalf, my testimony would not be valid. [32] But someone else is also testifying about me, and I assure you that everything he says about me is true. [33] In fact, you sent investigators to listen to John the Baptist, and his testimony about me was true. [34] Of course, I have no need of human witnesses, but I say these things so you might be saved. [35] John was like a burning and shining lamp, and you were excited for a while about his message. [36] But I have a greater witness than John—my teachings and my miracles. The Father gave me these works to accomplish, and they prove that he sent me. [37] And the Father who sent me has testified about me himself. You have never heard his voice or seen him face to face, [38] and you do not have his message in your hearts, because you do not believe me—the one he sent to you. [39] You search the Scriptures because you think they give you eternal life. But the Scriptures point to me!

37. **Malachi 4:5-6 NLT**— Look, I am sending you the prophet Elijah before the great and dreadful day of the Lord arrives. [6] His preaching will turn the hearts of fathers to their children, and the hearts of children to their fathers. Otherwise, I will come and strike the land with a curse.

38. **Numbers 11:26-29 NLT**— Two men, Eldad and Medad, had stayed behind in the camp. They were listed among the elders, but they had not gone out to the Tabernacle. Yet the Spirit rested upon them as well, so they prophesied there in the camp. [27] A young man ran and reported to Moses, "Eldad and Medad are prophesying in the camp!" [28] Joshua son of Nun, who had been Moses' assistant since his youth, protested, "Moses, my master, make them stop!" [29] But Moses replied, "Are you jealous for my sake? I wish that all the Lord's people were prophets and that the Lord would put his Spirit upon them all!"

PROPHET JESUS

Jesus is our very best example of a prophet. List a few examples of how He walked out His prophetic anointing.

_____
_____
_____
_____
_____
_____
_____

RESPONSIBILITY OVER GIFTING

Define what a *seer* is.

_____
_____
_____
_____
_____
_____

POWER-STEERING VERSUS SPIRIT-FILLED

What is the difference between an Old Testament prophet and a New Testament prophet?

_____
_____
_____
_____
_____
_____

JESUS TURNED ON THE LIGHTS

How did Jesus "turn the lights back on"?

_____

_____

_____

_____

_____

_____

A PROPHET BY DEFINITION

List the four operations on the prophetic spectrum and a brief description for each type.

_____

_____

_____

_____

_____

_____

_____

_____

_____

What have you learned from the portion included from Rick Renner's book _Apostles and Prophets?_ Was there something new that you hadn't known before? How has this new information informed your understanding about the office of the prophet?

_____

_____

_____

_____

_____

_____

_____

_____

SAILS CANNOT OPERATE
WITHOUT THE WIND

How does *the wind in the sails* apply to a real prophet receiving a word from the Lord?

_____

_____

_____

_____

_____

_____

DIFFERENT TYPES OF PROPHETS

What is the difference between the community church prophet-type and the John the Baptist-type of prophet?

_____

_____

_____

_____

_____

_____

JUDAS AND SILAS

How do we know that Judas and Silas were prophets? What was the fruit of their gifting?

_____

_____

_____

_____

_____

_____

MAJORS AND MINORS

What differentiates a major gift from a minor gift?

_____

_____

_____

_____

_____

_____

PROPHETS HEED
ONE ANOTHER'S WORDS

Mature prophetic figures should base everything on what two things?

_____

_____

_____

_____

_____

_____

WHAT PROPHETS DO

Describe what prophets *can* do.

_____

_____

_____

_____

_____

_____

_____

APOSTLES ARE CHOSEN, PROPHETS ARE GROWN

Explain the phrase "apostles are chosen, prophets are grown."

_____

_____

_____

_____

_____

_____

_____

_____

_____

_____

_____

THE SECRET TO THE LIFE OF JOHN

What was the *cup* that Jesus referenced in Mark 10:28-39, and how did James and John differ in the fulfillment of this question?

_____

_____

_____

_____

_____

_____

_____

_____

_____

_____

_____

FOCUS POINT

John was very aware of God's love for him. So much so that when writing about himself, he referred to himself as, "one of His disciples, whom Jesus loved." (*See* John 13:23.) This was one occasion that he labeled himself this. When we have a revelation of Jesus' love toward us, when the world sends us hardships, we will not be moved. Take this time to let the love of Jesus wash over you. Receive His love, be confident in His love, and write down what you experience in this time. (Meditate on John 3:16.)

PROPHETS ARE DIFFERENT

What can cause a prophet or apostle from being misunderstood or, even worse, misidentified?

_____

_____

_____

_____

_____

_____

_____

_____

_____

_____

PASTORS DON'T MAKE PROPHETS

What can be the result of mislabeling an office gift in the body?

_____

_____

_____

_____

_____

_____

_____

_____

_____

_____

_____

_____

APOSTLES' AUTHORITY

How has today's Church missed the prescription of building the Church the New Testament way?

_____

_____

_____

_____

_____

_____

_____

_____

_____

_____

HOW PROPHETS ARE CALLED—FOUR WITNESSES

How are prophets called, and what are the four qualifications they must have?

_____

_____

_____

_____

_____

_____

_____

_____

_____

_____

_____

_____

SPIRITUAL SONS OF THE PROPHETS

PERSONAL REFLECTION

Pursue love, and desire spiritual gifts, but especially that you may prophesy (1 Corinthians 14:1). Not everyone will work in the office of a prophet gifting; however, we can all prophesy. The Bible says we should desire the gift of prophecy. Take this personal reflection time to ask the Lord to teach you how He can use you according to Ephesians 4:11-12, and ask Him if He would like to give a word through you to someone.

CHAPTER TWENTY

A PROPHET'S REWARD

SCRIPTURES

1. **Romans 4:17**— (as it is written, "I have made you a father of many nations") in the presence of Him whom he believed—God, who gives life to the dead and calls those things which do not exist as though they did.

2. **Matthew 10:40-42**— He who receives you receives Me, and he who receives Me receives Him who sent Me. [41] He who receives a prophet in the name of a prophet shall receive a prophet's reward. And he who receives a righteous man in the name of a righteous man shall receive a righteous man's reward. [42] And whoever gives one of these little ones only a cup of cold water in the name of a disciple, assuredly, I say to you, he shall by no means lose his reward.

3. **First Samuel 9:6-10**— And he said to him, "Look now, there is in this city a man of God, and **he is an honorable man**; all that he says surely comes to pass. So let us go there; perhaps he can show us the way that we should go." [7] Then Saul said to his servant, "But look, if we go, what shall we bring the man? For the bread in our vessels is all gone, and there is no present to bring to the man of God. What do we have?" [8] And the servant answered Saul again and said, "Look, **I have here at hand one-fourth of a shekel of silver. I will give that to the man of God, to tell us our way.**" [9] (Formerly in Israel, when a man went to inquire of God, he spoke thus: "Come, let us go to the seer"; for he who is now called a prophet was formerly called a seer.) [10] Then Saul said to his servant, "Well said; come, let us go." So, they went to the city where the man of God was.

4. **First Samuel 7:7-10**— Now when the Philistines heard that the children of Israel had gathered together at Mizpah, the lords of the Philistines went up against Israel. And when the children of Israel heard of it, they were afraid of the Philistines. [8] So the children of Israel said to Samuel, "Do not cease to cry out to the Lord our God for us, that He may save us from the hand of the Philistines." [9] And Samuel took a suckling lamb and offered it as a whole burnt offering to the Lord. Then Samuel cried out to the Lord for Israel, and the Lord answered him. [10] Now as Samuel was offering up the burnt offering, the Philistines drew near to battle against Israel. But the Lord thundered with a loud thunder upon the Philistines that day, and so confused them that they were overcome before Israel.

5. **First Samuel 2:10**—The adversaries of the Lord shall be broken in pieces; from heaven He will thunder against them.

6. **Second Kings 4:42-44**—Then a man came from Baal Shalisha, and brought the man of God bread of the firstfruits, twenty loaves of barley bread, and newly ripened grain in his knapsack. And he said, "Give it to the people, that they may eat." [43] But his servant said, "What? Shall I set this before one hundred men?" He said again, "Give it to the people, that they may eat; for thus says the Lord: 'They shall eat and have some left over.'" [44] So he set it before them; and they ate and had some left over, according to the word of the Lord."

7. **Matthew 6:24**—No one can serve two masters; for either he will hate the one and love the other, or else he will be loyal to the one and despise the other. You cannot serve God and mammon.

8. **Proverbs 10:22**—The blessing of the Lord makes one rich, and He adds no sorrow with it.

9. **Matthew 17:27**—Nevertheless, lest we offend them, go to the sea, cast in a hook, and take the fish that comes up first. And when you have opened its mouth, you will find a piece of money; take that and give it to them for Me and you.

10. **Second Kings 6:5-6**—But as one was cutting down a tree, the iron ax head fell into the water; and he cried out and said, "Alas, master! For it was borrowed." [6] So the man of God said, "Where did it fall?" And he showed him the place. So he cut off a stick, and threw it in there; and he made the iron float.

11. **First Kings 17:10-24**—So he arose and went to Zarephath. And when he came to the gate of the city, indeed a widow was there gathering sticks. And he called to her and said, "Please bring me a little water in a cup, that I may drink." [11] And as she was going to get it, he called to her and said, "Please bring me a morsel of bread in your hand." [12] So she said, "As the Lord your God lives, **I do not have bread, only a handful of flour in a bin, and a little oil in a jar; and see, I am gathering a couple of sticks that I may go in and prepare it for myself and my son, that we may eat it, and die."** [13] And Elijah said to her, "Do not fear; go and do as you have said, but **make me a small cake from it first**, and bring it to me; and afterward make some for yourself and your son. [14] For thus says the Lord God of Israel: '**The bin of flour shall not be used up, nor shall the jar of oil run dry, until the day the Lord sends rain on the earth.'"** [15] So she went away and did according to the word of Elijah; and she and he and her household ate for many days. [16] **The bin of flour was not used up, nor did the jar of oil run dry, according to the word of the Lord** which He spoke by Elijah. [17] Now it happened after these things that **the son of the woman who owned the house became sick.** And his sickness was so serious that there was no breath left in him. [18] So she said to Elijah, "What have I to do with you, O man of God? Have you come to me to bring my sin to remembrance, and to kill my son?" [19] And he said to her, "Give me your son." So he took him out of her arms and carried him to the upper room where he was staying, and laid him on his own bed. [20] Then he cried out to the Lord and said, "O Lord my God, have You also brought tragedy on the widow with whom I lodge, by killing her son?" [21] And he stretched himself out on the child three times, and cried out to the Lord and said, "O Lord my God, I pray, let this child's soul come back to

him." [22] Then the Lord heard the voice of Elijah; and **the soul of the child came back to him, and he revived.** [23] And **Elijah took the child and brought him down from the upper room into the house and gave him to his mother.** And Elijah said, "See, your son lives!" [24] Then the woman said to Elijah, "Now by this I know that you are a man of God, and that the word of the Lord in your mouth is the truth."

12. **Acts 11:27-30**—And in these days prophets came from Jerusalem to Antioch. [28] Then one of them, named **Agabus, stood up and showed by the Spirit that there was going to be a great famine throughout all the world, which also happened in the days of Claudius Caesar.** [29] Then the disciples, each according to his ability, determined to send relief to the brethren dwelling in Judea. [30] This they also did, and sent it to the elders by the hands of Barnabas and Saul.

13. **Proverbs 22:3**—A prudent man foresees evil and hides himself, but the simple pass on and are punished.

14. **Hebrews 7:8**—Here mortal men receive tithes, but there he receives them, of whom it is witnessed that he lives.

15. **Second Chronicles 20:20**—So they rose early in the morning and went out into the Wilderness of Tekoa; and as they went out, Jehoshaphat stood and said, "Hear me, O Judah and you inhabitants of Jerusalem: **Believe in the Lord your God, and you shall be established; believe His prophets, and you shall prosper.**"

EZEKIEL AND THE VALLEY OF DRY BONES

The Voice of God is a multiplier; give a few examples from Scripture that show that He is a multiplier.

HONOR ENGAGES THE PROPHET'S REWARD

Explain the phrase, "Honor engages the prophet's reward." How can you apply this to your life?

_____

_____

_____

_____

_____

SAMUEL'S OBEDIENCE SAVES ISRAEL

It took one man's obedience to save Israel. Knowing the intensity of the situation, Samuel offered a burnt offering and interceded for the children of Israel. In our world today, what would be an offering that we could give while we intercede for others?

_____

_____

_____

_____

_____

GOD'S BEST WAS TO RULE THROUGH SAMUEL

Why do you think the people of Israel wanted a king when they had God Himself as their Defender? Do you think that this is still happening today? Give some examples.

_____

_____

_____

_____

_____

_____

_____

A GLIMPSE OF THE PROPHET'S REWARD

The prophet's reward in 1 Samuel 7:7-10 was God's supernatural protection and provision!

FOCUS POINT

Sometimes God will answer our request even if it is not entirely what He wants. Take this time right now to spend time with Him and pray that your desires line up with His desires. Write your prayer.

_____

_____

_____

_____

_____

_____

_____

_____

_____

_____

_____

_____

_____

_____

_____

_____

_____

_____

_____

_____

_____

_____

_____

SOWING WITH PROPER
MOTIVE INDUCES REWARD

Have you had moments of radical giving that stretched you to the point of concern? Write about it.

_____

_____

_____

_____

_____

_____

_____

_____

_____

_____

SOWING ACTIVATES GOD'S ECONOMY

When sowing into good soil, we know we will reap a good and plentiful harvest. Sowing into a prophet will reap a prophet's reward. Knowing this, in the moments that you have sown, what was the harvest or reward you received?

_____

_____

_____

_____

_____

_____

_____

_____

_____

_____

PROPHETS CARRY INCREASE

How has the idea of the prophet's reward changed or encouraged new mindsets for you and your future of sowing?

_____

_____

_____

_____

_____

_____

_____

_____

_____

_____

ALL SOIL IS NOT THE SAME

Sowing into the right soil can open a reward of the prophet's word to you, as well as other miraculous provisions. Knowing that all soil is not the same, have you given to different types of soil that have produced a different harvest? If so, write your experience.

_____

_____

_____

_____

_____

_____

_____

_____

_____

THE ANOINTING TO MULTIPLY

Supernatural multiplication is one of the gifts God has placed on His prophets. What are some things that you have seen or would like to see multiplied in your life?

_____

_____

_____

_____

_____

_____

_____

_____

_____

_____

WHAT BAAL SHALISHA REPRESENTS

Looking at what Baal Shalisha represents, why do you think it was significant that a man from Baal Shalisha brought the man of God an offering?

_____

_____

_____

_____

_____

_____

_____

_____

_____

_____

TRUE PROPHETS SOMETIMES SAY NO

Why do you think an aggressive prophetic giver will break off the demon of mammon?

_____

_____

_____

_____

_____

_____

_____

_____

_____

_____

_____

PERVERSION OF THE PROPHET'S REWARD

What are ways that show a prophet has a love for money?

_____

_____

_____

_____

_____

_____

_____

_____

_____

_____

_____

_____

THE DEVIL DOESN'T HAVE THE ANOINTING, SO HE USES MONEY

Give a brief description of what mammon is.

_____
_____
_____
_____
_____
_____
_____
_____
_____
_____

SOWING IS THE BEST RESPONSE TO TROUBLE OR CRISIS

It takes faith and obedience to sow, especially in times of hardship. During a hard season, have you been asked of the Lord to sow the last that you had? If so, what was the reward that you received from that sowing in a difficult time?

_____
_____
_____
_____
_____
_____
_____
_____
_____

THE PROPHET'S REWARD FOREWARNS CALAMITY

PERSONAL REFLECTION

When you release what you possess into the Kingdom, the possibilities for what God can do become limitless. The demon of mammon is fighting God's children and keeping them from sowing. Take this time to examine yourself and see if the demon of mammon has hindered you from being a generous sower and if it's blocking you from receiving the prophet's reward. Write your thoughts and prayer.

_____

_____

_____

_____

_____

_____

_____

_____

_____

_____

_____

_____

_____

_____

_____

_____

_____

_____

_____

_____

_____

_____

_____

CHAPTER TWENTY-ONE

DE-INSTITUTIONALIZING A REVELATION

SCRIPTURES

1. **Jeremiah 4:3**— For thus says the Lord to the men of Judah and Jerusalem: "Break up your fallow ground, and do not sow among thorns."

2. **Jeremiah 1:9-10**—Then the Lord put forth His hand and touched my mouth, and the Lord said to me: "Behold, I have put My words in your mouth. [10] See, I have this day set you over the nations and over the kingdoms, to root out and to pull down, to destroy and to throw down, to build and to plant."

3. **Revelation 2:4**— Nevertheless I have this against you, that you have left your first love.

4. **Acts 3:19**— Repent therefore and be converted, that your sins may be blotted out, so that times of refreshing may come from the presence of the Lord.

5. **Jeremiah 31:2-6 The Message**— This is the way God put it: "They found grace out in the desert, these people who survived the killing. Israel, out looking for a place to rest, met God out looking for them!" God told them, "I've never quit loving you and never will. Expect love, love, and more love! And so now I'll start over with you and build you up again, dear virgin Israel. You'll resume your singing, grabbing tambourines and joining the dance. You'll go back to your old work of planting vineyards on the Samaritan hillsides, and sit back and enjoy the fruit—oh, how you'll enjoy those harvests! The time's coming when watchmen will call out from the hilltops of Ephraim: 'On your feet! Let's go to Zion, go to meet our God!'"

6. **Jeremiah 31:3-6 NASB1977**— The Lord appeared to him from afar, saying, "I have loved you with an everlasting love; Therefore I have drawn you with lovingkindness. [4] Again I will build you and you will be rebuilt, O virgin of Israel! Again you will take up your tambourines, and go forth to the dances of the merrymakers. [5] Again you will plant vineyards on the hills of Samaria; the planters will plant and will enjoy them. [6] For there will be a day when watchmen on the hills of Ephraim call out, 'Arise, and let us go up to Zion, to the Lord our God.'"

7. **Jeremiah 29:11**— For I know the thoughts that I think toward you, says the Lord, thoughts of peace and not of evil, to give you a future and a hope.

8. **Mark 10:29-30**— So Jesus answered and said, "Assuredly, I say to you, there is no one who has left house or brothers or sisters or father or mother or wife or children or lands, for My sake and the gospel's, [30] who shall not receive a hundredfold now in this time—houses and brothers and sisters and mothers and children and lands, with persecutions—and in the age to come, eternal life."

9. **Hebrews 11:6**— But without faith it is impossible to please Him, for he who comes to God must believe that He is, and that He is a rewarder of those who diligently seek Him.

10. **Genesis 15:13-14**— Then He said to Abram: "Know certainly that your descendants will be strangers in a land that is not theirs, and will serve them, and they will afflict them **four hundred years**. [14] And also the nation whom they serve I will judge; afterward they shall come out with great possessions."

11. **Exodus 12:40-41 KJV**— Now the sojourning of the children of Israel, who dwelt in Egypt, was four hundred and thirty years. [41] And it came to pass at the end of the four hundred and thirty years, even the selfsame day it came to pass, that all the hosts of the Lord went out from the land of Egypt.

12. **Exodus 17:6**— "Behold, I will stand before you there on the rock in Horeb; and you **shall strike the rock,** and water will come out of it, that the people may drink." And Moses did so in the sight of the elders of Israel.

13. **Numbers 20:8-12**— Take the rod; you and your brother Aaron gather the congregation together. **Speak to the rock** before their eyes, and it will yield its water; thus you shall bring water for them out of the rock, and give drink to the congregation and their animals." [9] So Moses took the rod from before the Lord as He commanded him. [10] And Moses and Aaron gathered the assembly together before the rock; and he said to them, **"Hear now, you rebels! Must we bring water for you out of this rock?"** [11] Then **Moses lifted his hand and struck the rock twice with his rod; and water came out abundantly,** and the congregation and their animals drank. [12] Then the Lord spoke to Moses and Aaron, **"Because you did not believe Me, to hallow Me in the eyes of the children of Israel, therefore you shall not bring this assembly into the land which I have given them."**

14. **Mark 7:13**— **Making the word of God of no effect through your tradition** which you have handed down. And many such things you do.

15. **Exodus 18:21-22**— Moreover you shall select from all the people able men, such as fear God, men of truth, hating covetousness; and place such over them to be rulers of thousands, rulers of hundreds, rulers of fifties, and rulers of tens. [22] And let them judge the people at all times. Then it will be that every great matter they shall bring to you, but every small matter they themselves shall judge. So it will be easier for you, for they will bear the burden with you.

16. **Philippians 1:6**— Being confident of this very thing, that He who has begun a good work in you will complete it until the day of Jesus Christ.

TRIBES THAT LEAD TO MOVEMENTS

As we have learned, prophets are assigned to specific places, people groups, and leaders. Can you list a few prophets in today's world that are examples of this?

_____
_____
_____
_____
_____
_____
_____
_____
_____
_____

BREAKING UP FALLOW GROUND

What is needed from a prophet to break up hard ground and see a move of God?

_____
_____
_____
_____
_____
_____
_____
_____
_____
_____

DE-INSTITUTIONALIZING THE FIRST LOVE

FOCUS POINT

Revelation 2:4 says, "Nevertheless I have this against you, that you have left your first love." Remember back to when you first received Jesus as your Lord and Savior. Take this time to examine your life; do you feel that Revelation 2:4 is speaking to you? If so, take this time to remember where you were when you got saved and the fire and passion you had. Ask the Lord to reignite that same love and passion you once had. Write down your answer and prayer.

_____
_____
_____
_____
_____
_____
_____
_____
_____
_____
_____
_____
_____
_____
_____
_____
_____
_____
_____
_____
_____
_____

TIMES OF REFRESHING

Take this time to read Jeremiah 31:2-6. Write down the words the Lord speaks over you. He loves you so much.

_____

_____

_____

_____

_____

_____

_____

_____

_____

_____

OUTCASTS TURNED
INTO BROADCASTS

When you specifically give it all up for the Kingdom, He will make your life increase, and the anointing to take territory will follow you all the days of your life. Write down any way that Mark 10:29-30 applies to you.

_____

_____

_____

_____

_____

_____

_____

_____

_____

_____

DE-INSTITUTIONALIZING A REVELATION

DEVELOPING THE EXPRESSION
OF YOUR FAITH

How do you develop the expression of your faith?

_____

_____

_____

_____

_____

_____

_____

_____

_____

_____

_____

_____

WHAT IS AN EXPRESSION OF FAITH?

After reading the Hebrews Hall of Faith, which person in that list resonates with you and ministers to you?

_____

_____

_____

_____

_____

_____

_____

_____

_____

_____

_____

_____

_____

_____

MOSES WAS TEN YEARS PREMATURE

What lesson can be learned through the two examples that Joseph gave concerning Moses' actions that altered God's will for his life?

_____

_____

_____

_____

_____

_____

_____

_____

_____

_____

_____

INSTITUTIONALIZING A REVELATION

How does a revelation become institutionalized and what do we have to do to stop this from happening?

_____

_____

_____

_____

_____

_____

_____

_____

_____

_____

_____

FULFILLING YOUR PROPHETIC ASSIGNMENT

PERSONAL REFLECTION

God wants you to live, move, and have your being in Him. Take this final personal reflection time and write down what ministered to you the most in your reading of *Demystifying the Prophetic*. How are you going to apply what you have learned in your life starting today?

_____

_____

_____

_____

_____

_____

_____

_____

_____

_____

_____

_____

_____

_____

_____

_____

_____

_____

_____

_____

_____

_____

_____

_____

_____

DEAR READER

Dear reader, thank you for taking this journey with me in *Demystifying the Prophetic*. You mean more to the Kingdom of God than you might realize. Brand this into your heart.

A man or woman of God with a revelation is never at the mercy of a culture gone mad!

This is you, the one to whom God wants to give revelation. He desires that you receive His impartation of clarity and direction. You are, after all, part of His *ekklesia*—His only plan to change the world!

Thank you for joining me as we walked through this manual together.

Prophecy is a vast subject; I have desired to share it in a fresh and very grounded manner and in a way that causes it to be understandable and yet retains its power. God led you to walk through this manual; don't forget that. Take what you can and use it to serve your generation.

Dear reader, I love you, and as I write this, I'm praying for you. God knows you; God sees you and will finish what He started in you.

For Jesus,
Joseph Z

ABOUT THE AUTHOR

Joseph Z is an international prophetic voice who builds lives by the Word of God in the Church, government, and marketplace.

He is founder of the nonprofit organization Z Ministries, a parent entity for multiple conferences, specialized ministries, and social media events.

Joseph broadcasts *live* each weekday morning for one hour of teaching and prophetic ministry on the Joseph Z Facebook page and through JosephZ.com.

Joseph and his wife, Heather, have two amazing children, Alison and Daniel, and reside in the beautiful state of Colorado, USA.

From

JOSEPH Z

Thriving in God's Supernatural Economy

There's a war being fought over you! The Kingdom of God offers you divine provision while the Kingdom of Hell fights for territory in your life as a crisis looms on the world's horizon.

Will you break free of Hell's economy? International prophet and Bible teacher Joseph Z say it's urgent to break free now as we rapidly plunge into global difficulties involving worldwide market collapse, bank closures, a digital one-world currency, power grids failing, cyber war, medical deception, natural catastrophes, and unprecedented international conflict.

In *Breaking Hell's Economy,* Joseph makes it clear that we're at a destination in history that requires a revelation of God's supernatural economy—your ultimate defense against rising darkness.

Lay hold of this revelation, defy Hell, and live your life knowing you are destined to thrive in the last days!

Purchase your copy wherever books are sold

Joseph and Heather have ministered together for over 20 years; with a passion to see others be all they are called to be. For many years, Joseph & Heather have had the heart to offer life-changing materials and teaching at no cost to the body of Christ. Today, they have made that a reality by offering various media resources and biblical training free of charge. Joseph and Heather currently reside in Colorado Springs, CO with their two children, Alison and Daniel.

Learn more at
www.josephz.com

For Further Information

If you would like prayer or for further
information about Joseph Z Ministries,
please call our offices at

(719) 257-8050
or visit **josephz.com/contact**

Visit JosephZ.Com for additional materials

Stay Connected by Downloading the Joseph Z App

Search "Joseph Z" in your preferred app store.

Uncensored Truth

LIVE Chat

Prophetic Journalism

Real Time Prophetic Ministry

Interviews with Leading Voices

Video Archives

Equipping Believers to Walk in the Abundant Life

John 10:10b

Connect with us for fresh content and news about forthcoming books from your favorite authors...

Facebook @ HarrisonHousePublishers

Instagram @ HarrisonHousePublishing

www.harrisonhouse.com